THE RESILIENT SPIRIT

In memory of my father, Ercil Young, whose suffering brought me discernment

CONTENTS

Contents

ACKNOWLEDGMENTS

First and foremost, I am deeply grateful to Dan Gottlieb, Joanna Macy, June Singer, and Roshi Philip Kapleau—in the order their stories appear here—for their time and willingness to share their own stories of transformation. Many of my ideas for this book were only nascent when I interviewed them. Hearing their responses and commentaries on questions about suffering (the interview format appears in the appendix) was the start of a process of discovery. Working through the texts of their interviews and putting their reflections into a bigger context allowed me to reach beyond what I could have come to on my own.

Carol Foltz has been a thorough and conscientious research assistant on this project. She did a wonderful job of assembling the scholarly notes and references that appear in the endnotes. Without her help, I could not have identified the range of empirical support for resilience that appears here. Thank you, Carol.

Sue Trainor did an accurate and speedy job of word processing from the pages and notes and inserts that I assembled and reassembled. Thank you, Sue.

Acknowledgments

William Patrick and Sharon Broll have been extraordinary editors. I'm grateful for their insistent reorganization and trimming down of my rambling prose. This book has been a considerable reach for me, introducing for the first time some of my ideas and clinical experiences in a spiritual context. Often I was both too academic and too personal in my approach to these new topics. Without very active editors, I would have been lost.

During the writing of this book, my father died. He and I had had a complex and difficult relationship in life, but his dying transformed and simplified that relationship into new clarity and sweetness. He had a good death, and my experience of it deeply reinforced my belief in the transcendent coherence of human life—that what we're about is meaningful on many levels. I believe that death is a transition, a new development, both for the dying and for the living. I am everlastingly grateful for the experience of my father's death.

Nothing could be accomplished without my partner and husband, Ed Epstein. He remains my closest friend and collaborator in all that I do. He was deeply involved with this book, at first somewhat skeptically and later with a passion that surprised me. As always, I thank him for his time, energy, insight, and criticism.

Of course, in the end, I am accountable for what appears here. I hope that it conveys how suffering is linked to compassion, and why we should value suffering and pain as great (but difficult) teachers in the human realm.

INTRODUCTION

I have spent much of my life studying the problem of suffering. During childhood I was often confronted with misery and conflict as the adults around me seemed unable to hold together under the strain of poverty, family disputes, and fear. When I was an adolescent, I discovered my life's work: a search for reasons and cures for emotional and relational suffering. As an adult, I have invested thousands of hours in listening to people talk about their problems and the themes that revolve around them. As a psychologist, I study human development—in my own life, in my consulting room, and through empirical research.

I see now how I've benefited from a difficult childhood and how I was blessed with enough supports to transform its residues into knowledge and connection with others. I doubt that I could have chosen a more interesting life than the one I have if early privileges had been heaped on my plate or if I had been able to look ahead through a crystal ball. Working as a psychotherapist and psychoanalyst opens new horizons of meaning and insight every day of my life. Without the adversities of my childhood, how could I have awakened my curiosity about the purpose of human suffering at such an early time in my own life? This awakening led me to prepare for a career that teaches me to face the difficulties of life without despair. In observing, listening, studying the life-stories presented to me by people in pain, I have become increasingly more hopeful. What we seem to be learning is the transformation of adversity into purpose, of difficulty into development.

This book is about the "gifts"—insight, compassion, renewal—of suffering and pain. It is directed to the goal of understanding how and why adversity can sometimes lead to transformation and at other times only to more suffering. I draw on theories of development from psychology (especially Carl Jung), psychoanalysis, and Buddhism to unravel this mystery. I also draw on stories of resilience.

Because of my emphasis on resilience and renewal, I will not detail the pathological effects of trauma, abuse, or loss, although I'm fully aware of them. In my work as a Jungian analyst and psychologist, I've seen the undermining of trust, hope, and coherence that is the pathological by-product of trauma. In no way do I underestimate the waste of human life that results from direct and indirect abuse of children, from ignorance and oppression, and from the uneven distribution of material and educational resources in our society and in the world.

The notion that suffering includes gifts may seem an affront to people who believe that suffering and loss—especially among the poor and the ill and the oppressed—are simply unredeemable. I hope such people will read on, because they may see that sometimes even trauma can be converted into hope and meaning. Most of us need a lot of help and support to make that conversion. A few rare people do it quite on their own, as though they were equipped with an innate ability to see beyond or behind the wall of pain. Why shouldn't they be our teachers?

They have been mine. From the time I was a young child, I was captivated by the idea that suffering brings riches we could find in no other way—some insight or purpose. I was always searching for mentors who had survived catastrophe and benefited from it. As a child of eight or nine, I came up with my own theory of the creative personality, akin to the now generally outmoded belief that childhood difficulties may produce later artistic or humanistic achievements. In my work as a psychotherapist over the past twenty years, I've been inspired by Jung's idea that "lead" can be turned into "gold" in the process of adult development. Childhood adversity, the mess of marital conflicts, and injury or illness often rouse us to ask questions that will eventually lead to a sense of purpose, through new self-awareness and insight. Spiritual practices and knowledge have assisted human beings in the process of transforming lead into gold over millenia.

Buddhism has been a major source of inspiration in my life from the time even before I went to graduate school for training in psychology. For many years I didn't talk about my Buddhist background publicly, in part for fear it would alienate people from me, that it would be viewed as too exotic. Now that Buddhism has a wide following in the West, and is available in readable translations to many, I think it is time to credit it directly in the perspective I take.

Introduction

Many people have helped in putting this book together, but those whose stories are told in detail have been essential. Without their stories, there would be no book. Because psychotherapy is confidential, I cannot draw directly on the stories I hear in therapy. It could easily wound my clients and destroy their trust were I to tell their stories to others. I do use composite images of clients and give them names and personalities to bring them to life, but they're still somewhat fictional. Nor can I draw fully on my own life story—although I tell bits of it—because in my work as an analyst I need to maintain a certain degree of anonymity. My clients should be able to leave behind any concerns about my history and remain directly involved with their own. Because of the constraints due to my work, I had to look beyond the life stories immediately available to me. What I found are tales of resilience and renewal, of transformation through pain and suffering.

The detailed examples you'll read here are the stories of four dear friends of mine. Throughout the book I'll introduce their experiences and accounts, collected in a four-hour interview for this project, that show us the details of transformation. (They've read and approved everything that I say about them.) I'll also be telling the major events of their lives that relate to their transformation, so that you can see overall how pain and suffering entered and were woven into their accomplishments. Their lives are inspirational gifts to us all.

PART ONE

The Gifts

Many years ago I saw a couple in psychotherapy who had lost a young child to a protracted serious illness. During one session the child's father told me a story about an old Chinese sage that had helped him enormously during his grief. He had discovered it by chance in a 1946 detective novel.

Renowned as a wise man who was filled with a zest for life and for life's adventures, the sage had one odd habit that provoked curiosity among the people. He always rode his mule backwards.

Frequently people asked him, "Why do you ride your mule backwards?"

He would respond, "In life, it makes no difference where one is going. The destination is unimportant. It is only what one does along the way that counts."

Pressing him further, they would say, "So how should we respond to life?"

"Do not become swollen with pride at triumph or despondent over defeat. Good fortune or bad fortune is unimportant. The vicissitudes of life are but the means to shape your character. If you suffer adversity and react in the proper way, in the long run you will be benefited as fully as though you had good fortune. Cooperate with Destiny to strengthen your character by whatever experience life has to offer."

The old man was indifferent to wealth, fame, and failure. He rode backwards so that he would pay less attention to what was happening to him and more attention to his own reactions.

When I heard this story, I was impressed by its wisdom and the comfort it had provided my client. I was doubly impressed by the way he had found it. Just when this young man thought his situation was overwhelming, he found that this story could help him make sense out of his pain and see it as an opportunity for new development within himself.

Everything that I offer here, in the way of specifics and advice and story about how suffering can be beneficial, could be summarized by saying "Ride your mule backwards." To unpack that idea, we'll need to spend a few hundred pages together.

YOU MAY BE READING this book because you're in pain. Or you may have picked it up because you've survived adversity, recently or in childhood. This is a book about facing adversity, transforming it into discovery and development. All of us face hardship in our lives, but most of us are in fast retreat from the pain and suffering connected to it.

THE GIFTS

We believe that we should be able to rid ourselves of pain. We think that suffering is a waste of time. In our society we are surrounded by antisuffering campaigns in which we're encouraged to try to protect ourselves by assuming the illusion of control. Making more money, lessening our dependence on substances or people, altering our moods with antidepressants, and focusing more and more on success and competence, we lure ourselves into false securities. Some say we should simply eliminate whatever hurts: an illness, a spouse, depression, duty, work.

In the meantime we forget that suffering is an essential part of the human condition, one of the engines of human development. The unavoidable mysteries of pain and suffering can give rise to hidden resources of compassion and creativity. Until we reach our limits, we don't know how to overcome them. Until we feel our greatest fears directly, we don't know our courage. It is only when adversity has knocked our defenses down that we pose the big questions: Who am I? What is my purpose here? It is in times of need that we break habitual barriers between ourselves and others and experience intimate connections, often for the first time.

Until a couple of years ago, I would have declined to write about suffering, seeing it as beyond my ken. Suffering and its meanings have traditionally been the province of religion. But I have seen too many people with no appreciation of their suffering, no clue about how or why it might be meaningful. Too often in initial meetings of psychotherapy when I ask about a mother or a father, I hear a rote response: "I came from a dysfunctional family" or "My mother was an alcoholic." When I ask for more—"Give me a bigger picture;

what was your father like as a person?"—I often get a perplexed and even peeved look back. "I don't remember much, but the most important thing was that he was very distant. I played out the role of the communicator/peacemaker/pleaser—whatever—in my family." Similarly, when I meet people in professional or social situations, their views on adversity are often confused or limited. The death of a spouse or loved one feels like only an unredeemable loss. A divorce has no meaning other than a "mistake" or the symptom of dysfunctionality. Rather than mining these losses and tragedies for the richness they teach about ourselves and about the nature of being human, many of us too quickly label them and dismiss them or hide them in shame and fear.

We also tend to believe that the struggles of childhood boil down to a simple formula: if we're not thriving as adults, then our parents must have been abusive or alcoholic or ignorant. Or the reverse—if our parents were abusive or alcoholic or ignorant, then we cannot thrive as adults. Sadly, this formula cheats us of the complexity and compassion that bring nuance and discovery to our understanding of ourselves and others.

Although traditional psychotherapy and its tracing of difficulty back to childhood may have encouraged us to complain openly about our parents, we often seem to have missed the deeper lessons. Both Freud and Jung founded their therapies on the premise that remembering and facing what has been most traumatic or painful is the beginning of health. When we try to avoid or deny what troubles us, we're generally in for more trouble. Neat labels that seem to place blame elsewhere may be a form of avoiding responsibility for our attitudes and actions. Fantasies of overcoming our difficulties, of finally defeating illness or loss or death, become barriers to knowing ourselves and others. We feel alienated and adrift.

Many theories of development and spirituality draw some kind of distinction between useful suffering, which leads to development, and useless suffering, which leads merely to the repetition of suffering. Carl Jung talked about neurotic suffering as a bogus replacement for real suffering. In his writings he clearly separated the repetitive ruminations, worries, self-doubts, and anxious habits of the neurotic from the suffering that is an essential part of life. Honest confrontation with this deeper anguish over our ordinary human limitations and imperfections, our inevitable loss, illness, decline, and death, wakes us to the significance of our lives.

Neurosis is a barrier to encountering fully the meaning in our pain. Neurosis distracts and deludes us through idealism and grand expectations, self-pity and envy. It binds us to a childish perspective—demanding that things be as we would like them, ashamed and enraged when they are not.

Until we take responsibility for our own subjective lives— our attitudes and actions—we remain neurotic children repeating the mistakes we learned in our childhood and blaming others for our faults. Jung believed that we reinforce neurotic strivings in some of our Western religious beliefs because we enthrone our god as an eternal parent. People who regard divinity primarily as a powerful protector never mature. They *"remain* children instead of becoming *as* children, and they do not gain their life because they have not lost it."* The notion of "losing" one's life means being forced to let go of childish wishes for control and perfection and to encounter directly the challenges of pain and difficulty in our lives. Those childish wishes are reflected in contemporary antisuffering campaigns that say loss, illness, old age—maybe even death—can be overcome by some kind of scientific or spiritual manipulation.

An ancient tradition of distinguishing between pain and suffering exists in Buddhism, a religion that has been exploring this distinction for more than twenty-five hundred years. Buddhism offers perhaps the most developed account of human suffering and its meaning because its founder took as his central mission the alleviation of suffering. Its teachings contain psychological insight and practical wisdom about the transformation of difficulty into development.

If you have no acquaintance with Buddhism, it may seem to be an exotic or even alien perspective. But if you can open your mind to seeing what this ancient yet contemporary religion says about your life, I think you'll find that it helps in some remarkably specific ways. I draw on Buddhism here because of my personal experience with it, which I'll discuss soon, and because of its enormous helpfulness in responding to the problem of suffering at all levels of existence, from everyday complaints to confrontations with painful illness and death.

I'll give only a brief introduction to Buddhism because you will discover more about its significance in seeing how it illuminates the issues surrounding human difficulty. *Buddha* is a Sanskrit word that has two related meanings. It means (1) ultimate Truth or Mind and (2) one who is awakened to the true nature of existence. The person known as Buddha, an

Indian prince born more than twenty-five hundred years ago, had been prophesied to be a leader of a small kingdom but chose instead to follow a spiritual path. Prince Siddhartha, as he was known before he became enlightened, is said to have chosen a spiritual life specifically because he was so distressed by poverty, illness, and old age.

The India of his period had a strong caste system. The very lowest caste, the Untouchables, worked exclusively at tasks that no one else would perform: moving dead bodies to funerary pyres, cleaning up human and animal waste, fending off poisonous snakes and other dangerous animals from human living spaces, and so on. Siddhartha, from the most privileged ruling caste, was deeply perturbed by the plight of the Untouchables. He could not accept the conventional religious teaching, that these people had been born into their caste as a result of previous lives and could not change their circumstances until a next lifetime.

Siddhartha also observed that regardless of one's rank in life or one's spiritual attainments, everyone in this world is subject to illness, pain, loss, and death. These conditions provoked strong spiritual yearnings in this young prince. He wanted to discover the causes or origins of suffering so that he could find a cure. After six years of following the austere and demanding yogic practices of his day, Siddhartha was weak and exhausted. In a moment of inspiration, he discovered what he called the "middle way" of meditative practice, a method that fostered good health and physical strength, as well as concentration and mindfulness. Through this method, Siddhartha eventually attained a profound recognition of the nature of human life.

Fundamentally, he saw how we create suffering and how we can alleviate it. He saw also, concretely and specifically, the interwoven connection of all beings in this world, joined through their dependence on each other. Seeing these truths clearly, he also saw how human life can be great agony or great joy and opportunity. To live a life of freedom, health, and joy, we must be compassionate and tolerant. To become compassionate and tolerant, as we shall see, entails our own individual confrontation with pain and suffering, the penetration of their meaning and the awakening to our dependence, our interconnection with all beings. The Buddha taught a method for developing this process and left behind him a vast body of knowledge and wisdom from his own experience.

After his enlightenment, the Buddha spent forty-five years traveling and teaching. Many of his myriad teachings have been recorded, and his legacy is immense. I'll draw on only a few of his teachings that are central to understanding how to transform pain, adversity, and suffering into development and creativity. I'll use images and ideas from Buddhism, but not the religion as a whole.

One central idea is contained in the Sanskrit word *dukkha*, a term used by the Buddha to describe the fundamental condition of human life. This term is usually translated into English as "suffering," but it would be better translated as "dissatisfaction" or "discontent." The word literally means a wheel not running on its axle or a bone that has slipped out of its socket. You can think of dukkha as the reactions or internal commentaries that are activated by unpleasant or painful situations. The "I don't like this" or "Why is this happening to me?" or "Why am I so stupid?" kind of either imperceptible or well-known attitude that we take when things aren't going as we would like. The idea of dukkha will be the core of how we understand suffering here, as we explore the difference between pain and suffering. It is similar to what Jung meant when he said that neurosis is useless suffering; dukkha is friction and discontent, negativity that keeps us off balance, bound to our wishes and complaints. Pain, on the other hand, is a necessary and universal condition of being human. The human life cycle of birth, development, decline, and death includes much pain and loss that are unavoidable. When understood well, painful experiences awaken us to new meaning and purpose. When dukkha—neurosis or suffering—interferes with our encounters with pain (as it inevitably will), then we are thrown off course in our development, often stuck in self-pity, envy, and resentment that lead to more suffering and can even create more pain if we act on them.

The first major tenet of Buddhism is that "life is suffering," in the sense of dukkha. Incompleteness, dissatisfaction, and confusion are to be expected in human life, but they can be alleviated and transformed. Often we don't notice our incompleteness until we experience pain or sorrow that arouses our awareness. For some of us, the awareness of life's incompleteness comes from adversity in childhood; for others, from illness or loss or betrayal later. However it is aroused, when we begin to notice that we are not in control, that bad things happen no matter how much we try to be good and plan for the future, we are thrown into a noticeable state of dukkha—incompleteness, dissatisfaction, and confusion.

THE GIFTS

Buddhism teaches that much of our suffering is the direct consequence of our own (often unacknowledged) beliefs and attitudes that are carried over into our perceptions and actions. This is exactly what Jung and Freud discovered in their early investigations of the unconscious and exactly what I see repeatedly in my work and life. By drawing on scientific research, psychology, Jung's theories, and Buddhism, I hope to offer a guide from diverse sources—some contemporary and some ancient—that will point the way clearly from useless to useful suffering. Along this path lie the gifts that lead us from pain to transformation.

MY STORY

ACCORDING TO BUDDHISM, the only way to alleviate suffering is to dissolve our wishes for control, our self-protectiveness, and the separateness that we feel from others. Certain ingredients must be present for adversity to be transformed into the gifts of insight, compassion, and renewal. They can be understood only in the context of actual lives, and for that reason this book contains the stories of many people. Their stories tell us how we transform difficulty into discovery, but ultimately each of us must do this for ourselves.

As this is my book, it is in many ways my story. That I'm writing a book about suffering is not surprising. My childhood presented many occasions to witness suffering, pain, aggression, and violence. Perhaps because I was not often the victim, but rather the observer, I had ample time to see, contemplate, and try to figure out why life contained so much misery.

A background misery pervaded my rural, isolated early childhood. From the age of three or four on, I was often wrenched out of daydreams and playtime activities by people screaming. Mostly I saw and heard my parents fighting, sometimes other relatives.

In today's parlance some of these scenes would come under the rubric of domestic violence. When I was growing up, there was no name for these frightening disputes. To some extent they were a way of life in my own and others' homes, expected skirmishes in the battle between the sexes, between parents and children. When I heard stories about "the war," about the Germans and the Japanese, I related them to the conflicts I saw at home and in my neighborhood. As a small child, I had grand, comforting fantasies of speaking from a soapbox to large crowds, saying: "You must stop. No ideal or belief is important enough to warrant these hatreds." I was a very serious child.

The mystery surrounding suffering perturbed me. Even when life was pleasant (and it often was in our tidy little house close to nature), I was afraid and worried. Why did my elders inflict such miseries on each other, and sometimes on their children? Why were some people so easy to distress and so difficult to soothe?

From about the age of four on, I was always in some way preoccupied with questions about why we suffer. As a young child, I thought the answer was ignorance. Most people couldn't see the simple truth that we should love and protect one another. As I grew older, the simple truth faded and was replaced by theories and ideas about the complexity of human beings and life itself. For some reason, peculiar to me no doubt, I never considered natural disasters or accidents to be in the realm of suffering, in my childhood perspective. The workings of nature seemed to me "fair" and "just" based not on human justice or needs but on some system apart from humanity. The suffering I knew was the product of what human beings did to each other, themselves, and the living world around them. Later when I learned the term *evil*, I assessed humans as the agents of evil. The devil theory never made any sense to me. Nor did it make sense to say that an illness, a flood, a poisonous snake, or a virus is evil. Those natural events seemed to follow different laws, something beyond good and bad. The factor I connected to suffering as a child, and to evil later, was the way in which people made misery by resenting, hating, belittling, and demeaning themselves, their lives, and others.

By the time I was eight or nine, I could see that my parents were disappointed in me. I was too studious. I was unathletic. I was often very quiet, sometimes anxious and withdrawn. Several adults outright told me that I was too serious, and others just tried to cheer me up. People would say the 1950s equivalent of "Lighten up": "Why have you got the worries of the world on your shoulders?"

I wondered why I was so heavyhearted. I clearly had food, clothes, lots of animals I loved, beautiful fields and woods, a few friends, and fairly good health. Why was I so frequently anxious and so "unable to be a child," as the grown-ups put it?

When I was eight or nine, I made an accidental discovery. I was reading through the classics section (A to Z, in order) of the public library with a burning desire to *know* about human life. I was often entertained and delighted by the books I read, and yet I typically devoured them with a searching seriousness and a tendency to make copious notes (considered bizarre in my family, which did not see reading as a pastime and viewed it suspiciously: "What are you *doing* in that bedroom?"). I noticed that the biographical summaries, or the stories themselves, revealed that the writers had had difficult and sometimes tragic childhoods. It dawned on me that my superseriousness was okay: a difficult childhood sometimes leads to some great discovery or work of art or ability to write in adulthood. I determined to make use of the suffering I had witnessed, and I have.

When I look back over my development as a person and a therapist, I realize that nine-tenths of what has been important or essential was related to pain and suffering in some way. On the surface perhaps it sounds morbid, but I often value what's negative and difficult more than what is easy and comfortable. And I'm not a masochist. It's just that our difficult circumstances and negative emotions keep us awake far more fully than any pleasures do. If I had grown up in a situation of privilege and easy communication, I doubt that I would have undertaken to work with and study suffering— that I would have been attracted to much of what I cherish most in life, including Buddhism and Jung's psychology.

Turning Lead into Gold

Since those first forays into the library, I've delved quite a bit more into theories of human development. In graduate school I picked up a very different picture of early hardship. According to the tenets of developmental psychology, not only does a difficult childhood lead to very little creativity and much psychopathology, but the security of a happy bond to one or both parents is the best promissory note for later achievements that parents can give. Nothing good can come from conflicts at home or anxiety about one's parents. Every author from Sigmund Freud to Erik Erikson, and then later from John Bowlby to Daniel Stern, stressed the crucial importance of happy, secure attachments in childhood. It is this grounding, they argued, that leads to the kind of confident autonomy that produces success in adulthood.

One prominent exception to this prevailing view was that of Carl Jung. He spoke of the theme of transformation, of developing through difficulty into greater integration, and used the alchemical metaphor of transforming lead into gold.

The American psychiatrist Harry Stack Sullivan was another contrarian voice. He stressed the importance of peer relationships—our childhood and adolescent chums—over and above what parents alone can provide. He believed that each of us gets a new opportunity to revise identity and development at each new stage of life, based on the ways our friends can offer honest, authentic feedback and reflections.

The psychoanalyst Heinz Kohut talked about the advantages that adversities can bring in childhood, provided the personality is strong enough to survive them and keep going. Well-timed adversities that don't overwhelm can strengthen our belief in ourselves as resilient and self-determining.

Jung, Sullivan, and Kohut were the theorists I found most refreshing and hopeful in my early encounters with models of human development. I was motivated by a psychology of the underdog, so to speak, hungry for any sign of hope for the poor and disadvantaged, the oppressed and abused. I was also fascinated by the ways in which people endure and transform suffering.

Since my graduate school days, things have changed a great deal in regard to the topic of resilience. *Resilience* is now a new term in psychology, defined as the ability to thrive, not just survive, after having encountered some great difficulty or adversity. Although success is defined in many ways, people who are resilient count themselves as "successful." For some this means the confidence to overcome any obstacle that emerges.

A middle-aged African American woman, quoted in a study of resilient black adults, said: "Success means, no matter what obstacle you face, it should only be a temporary stumbling block. You should find some way to remove it or go around it, no matter what. . . ." However success is defined, the earmark of the resilient is that they feel *good* about who they are and what they're doing.

In the past fifteen years or so, resilience has emerged from a tiny corner of psychological studies of children of deeply disturbed, often schizophrenic, parents to the mainstream of psychological research. Still, though, it presents many puzzles to researchers and observers. Why do some people respond to suffering by transforming themselves, finding new meanings, becoming compassionate? Why do other people respond by falling apart, stagnating, protecting themselves, and eventually becoming bitter, enraged, envious?

No one disagrees about the enormous importance of consistent, caring, sustaining, and empathic parenting, especially in early life when children are so vulnerable. If children receive this kind of care and love, they will lastingly benefit from it. But what about the millions of children who do not grow up in caring, secure environments? Are they doomed to weakness and insufficiency? Can we change ourselves through encounters with adversity and develop ourselves even though parents and other caregivers failed us?

On the other hand, if childhood provides security and love and sustenance, how does one encounter the necessary failures and losses and adversities that adulthood brings? Is a child from a loving, caring family prepared to endure and transform the betrayal of a spouse, serious illness, or a disabling accident? What prepares a person to be resilient in adulthood?

As we will see throughout this book, the capacity to be resilient, to respond to difficulty with development, is rooted in many diverse factors, but it consistently depends on *one* thing: the meaning you, the individual, make of where you are. When suffering leads to meanings that unlock the mysteries of life, it strengthens compassion, gratitude, joy, and wisdom. When suffering leads to barriers and retaliations and hatred, it empties you of hope and love, and then misery will lead to misery, the drama that I witnessed all too often in my childhood.

A contemporary researcher of resilience says this: "The voices of the resilient send a powerful message: personal perceptions and responses to stressful life events are crucial elements of survival, recovery, and rehabilitation, often transcending the reality of the situation or the interventions of others." Like the Chinese sage riding backwards, the resilient pay more attention to their attitudes and reactions than to the actual events that trouble them.

Resilience is neither a single action nor a constant state. But I have learned that it can be promoted by the actions that we take, and that it does not need to remain the mystery that it seemed to me for so much of my life.

I have personally witnessed people returning to engage with life after facing betrayal, cancer, AIDS, the death of a child, the Holocaust, abandonment, and childhood abuse and neglect. The resilient have returned to life enriched with knowledge and wisdom and renewed concern for others. I've seen the opposite as well: people who have been defeated by calamity or, worse yet, negatively transformed into vengeful, resentful, envious, hateful victims.

What seems to matter in encountering the difficult circumstances of our lives is not so much the quality of the event itself (the degree of pain, loss, or humiliation) but the attitude or meaning that one brings to the event. We create heaven or hell through our own responses.

We all struggle to avoid hell and to find heaven, but we may be ignorant of how much power is in our own hands. There is a famous story in Zen Buddhism about a samurai who confronted a Zen master.

"You're supposed to be a great Zen master," said the samurai. "So I want you to tell me the truth about heaven and hell. Do they really exist?"

Without a moment's hesitation, the master responded, "What, even such an ugly and untalented man as you can become a samurai? Amazing!"

Immediately the proud samurai became enraged and drew his sword. "I'll kill you!" he roared.

Fearlessly, the master said, "This is hell."

The samurai paused and grew thoughtful. His face softened from its angry scowl. Sheathing his sword, he put his hands together palm to palm and bowed before the master.

"And this," said the master, just as calmly, "is heaven."

Unknowingly we bring much greater suffering to ourselves than any event or situation could deliver in and of itself. And yet we also have the capacity to bring great peace and calm.

WHY LIFE IS INTERESTING

THE OBVIOUS TRUTH about suffering is that we don't have to go out of our way to encounter it. It is not the stuff that we have to seek on the mountain top or shop for in expensive stores. It is absolutely unavoidable in the design of life, and the sooner we discover its value, the better we're able to know who we are.

Buddhism offers an image known as the Wheel of Life. It is represented as a mandala or circle filled with depictions of six realms of existence that show all that is possible in forms of life. Each realm is regarded as both a psychological state and a "place" or situation.

The lowest realm is hell. In it are forms of existence that are bound to fear and aggression in which beings are thrust from one state of pain to another because they do not recognize how they are creating these states within themselves. The key to getting out of a hellish existence is to look into the mirror and recognize oneself as the author; this is why the saintly figure (*bodhisattva* in Sanskrit) who guards this realm is depicted as holding a mirror in his hand.

There is a belief that the hell realm, although excruciating, can lead to enlightenment or awakening more directly than can heaven, in which one feels comfortable and satisfied. In heaven one can easily slip into unconsciousness, lack of mindfulness, but in hell one is always alert because of the pain. The belief in the value of pain and suffering is expressed in many religions and myths, often in terms of the importance of a descent into the underground or the entrance into the cave of the dragon.

The author and social and environmental activist Joanna Macy is a professor of systems theory and deep ecology at the Graduate Theological Union in Berkeley and the California Institute of Integral Studies in San Francisco. She is internationally known for organizing "despair and empowerment" workshops and conferences in which people confront their feelings about some of the overwhelming problems of our present and future. When she talks about the necessity of facing the pain of the contemporary world, the ways in which poverty and crime and our overcompetitive economic system snag us into constant suffering, she recalls her first spiritual awakening to the importance of accepting suffering: "It was in relation to the crucifixion where I saw God as being able to encompass human suffering. He was demonstrating that. That He would be actually hammered up on a cross wasn't indulging in any sugarcoating. It was an acknowledgment of our suffering, but it was also a statement that you go through it and get transformed."

The value of suffering in our own development is a component of all major religions, but its significance seems to have faded in the late twentieth century. Many of our spiritual and psychological leaders speak as though our goal is simply to overcome difficulties. Joanna says that she is sometimes in dialogue with spiritual teachers who feel she overemphasizes the darker, destructive side of contemporary life. She responds to them by saying: "It's important to me to go into hell, to feel how I suffer with our world, in a way that can be walked into and talked about. This opens us to our compassion and teaches us about our interdependence."

Throughout the rest of the book, we'll examine the exact steps taken by some who have made the journey from suffering and pain to compassion and creativity. In Part Two, I'll discuss some of the specific details of the map I've made from my own and others' experiences. But for now, here is what the Jungian analyst and author June Singer (whose story we shall explore) said when I asked her about her advice to others in confronting pain or loss: "Whether it's physical, emotional, whatever kind of pain, don't storm against it. Don't resist it with questions like, Why me? Why this? Instead say to yourself, This is what the situation is. This is where I am and this is what is happening right now. What can I make of this? How can I deal with it? How must I change? How can I change the situation? You really have to take it on, without deluding yourself, without denying how hard it is; that's what I've learned about pain."

So if you've just encountered a painful situation, or if you're looking back, trying to make sense of something that happened a while ago, simply notice the difficulty and your reactions to it. The next step is to begin to understand those reactions so that you can reduce your suffering and allow the process of transformation to unfold.

PART TWO

Suffering and Compassion

If anybody achieves at least endurance of misery, he has already accomplished an almost superhuman task.

CARL JUNG, 1937

PAIN, LOSS, ILLNESS, AND DEATH are fundamental features of our existence that guarantee that we change or revise ourselves from time to time. They bring up questions of purpose and meaning, and in this way they make our lives more interesting and challenging.

But they are not the same as *suffering* in the way I'm talking about it here. Suffering is the discontent, the negativity or dissatisfaction that we often feel, sometimes in relation to pain or loss but also in response to ordinary hassles in life, such as a traffic jam or a bounced check. Suffering is the negative commentary and grumbling—the background noise that accompanies many of us in everyday life.

I mentioned earlier, the First Noble Truth of Buddhism is translated as "Life is suffering." When Westerners hear this idea, we frequently miss its wisdom and reject it as depressing or life-despising. Nothing could be further from its actual meaning. It alerts us to pay attention to the ways in which we normally react to the world around us so that we can free ourselves from our constant evaluations and negativity. It is riding the mule backwards. Buddhism asks us to focus on our own reactions and perspective, the ways we create distress rather than respond simply to what's going on. When a person is unself-consciously engaged in the moment, there is no grumbling, no commentary, no holding back.

Mihalyi Csikszentmihalyi, a psychologist of human development from the University of Chicago, discovered evidence to support the First Noble Truth of Buddhism. He calls the connection to the present moment "flow" experience. He has found large amounts of flow in chess playing, mountain climbing, surgery, dancing, painting, music, and many other concentrated activities—and some of it in all of us from time to time. Engaged in flow experience, people are unconcerned about the final goal. They are riding the mule without a thought to where they are going. In such a state, everyone reports being absolutely content and alert—calm and focused. Unfortunately, flow is rare for most of us.

Trying to understand why flow is so difficult to achieve and why so many of us feel deprived of it, Csikszentmihalyi found that, in general, human beings' thoughts and consciousness are chaotic and negative:

> It could be argued that chaos, not order, is the natural state of mind. When no external stimulation engages attention . . . thoughts begin to drift randomly. Instead of a pleasant, logical thread of mental experiences, disconnected ideas appear out of nowhere, and even if we make an effort to

do so, it is impossible to return to a coherent line of thought for more than a few minutes.

Meditators know this from their own experience, but people who have never tried meditating may feel that they are personally "attention deficient" because they are so distractible and unable to focus most of the time. For people in general, only concentration relieves this experience of ordinary mental chaos. When we're working at something that absorbs our attention or we're involved in a ritual or doing some other kind of structured activity, we automatically direct our thoughts and we feel better. At most other times, we are held hostage to the jumbled array of unfocused stuff that rolls through our minds.

In addition to the chaotic and random qualities of our ordinary thoughts, our natural attitude is quite negative: "The roaming mind usually attends to negative thoughts" and "such a pessimistic bias might be adaptive—if by 'adaptation' we mean an increased likelihood of survival. The mind turns to negative possibilities as a compass needle turns to the magnetic pole, because this is the best way, on the average, to anticipate dangerous situations."

This natural dissatisfaction, as the Buddha discovered in his awakening to the true nature of our lives, is always in the background for humans. It is probably connected with our being constantly alert to an opportunity to improve things, a sort of instinctual negativity that leads to greater and greater competence. Such a generally negative attitude may be useful for the species as a whole but is often problematic for the individual. It disrupts our ability to concentrate directly on our actions and tends to keep our attention on evaluations of whether or not we like what's happening.

Buddhists talk about suffering as that which separates us from engaging in our immediate experience. It sets us apart and can keep us apart from others. Commentaries like "why me?" or "poor me" or "stupid me" are symptoms of suffering. These thoughts and feelings pull us into agitations and annoyance. Surprisingly, suffering is often more disturbing than the original pain itself. The following story reminds me of myself in many situations when my own thoughts and feelings have caused me greater distress than were called for.

One evening, a man was invited to the home of a friend. As he was about to drink a cup of tea, he thought he saw a baby snake in the cup! He did not want to embarrass his hostess, so he gathered all of his courage and swallowed the tea in one gulp.

After returning home later that night, he began to feel severe pains in his stomach. By the next day, the pains had grown worse. He consulted several doctors and tried many cures, but none worked. The man, now seriously ill, thought he was about to die.

Hearing of his condition, his friend invited him to tea again. Sitting in the same spot as earlier, the man accepted a cup of tea. When he looked down to drink it, suddenly he saw the snake again. This time he drew his hostess's attention to it. Without a word, she pointed to the ceiling above him. He looked up. There, hanging from a beam, was a length of rope. The sick man realized that the "baby snake" had been a reflection of rope. The two friends looked at each other and laughed. The sick man's pain vanished instantly, and he recovered perfect health.

SUFFERING AND COMPASSION

Suffering always involves a fantasy, a fear, a thought, or a commentary interjected between ourselves and our experiences. Whether our pain is real or entirely imagined, the fantasy and fears about the pain can hold our attention and keep us feeling off center and isolated. This interjection of discontent or fear between an experience and its meaning creates the misery that stagnates us. When you notice how you do this, you begin to see how much misery you create in addition to whatever necessary pain or loss you must endure. Through the acceptance and understanding of actual pain, we begin to develop the knowledge and compassion that are the unspoken benefits of adversity. Dukkha, or the fantasies and fears about pain, can arrest us in our ability to become conscious and make transformative use of pain.

Jung talks about neurosis as this kind of unnecessary suffering. It imposes a childish perspective—for example, of helplessness or powerlessness—on an adult experience of stress, frustration, challenge, or difficulty. We impose this perspective on our relationships and problems by assuming that life should automatically go our way or that we've been victimized when it doesn't. It's not that we literally think like children, but that we don't take full responsibility for ourselves. We believe that others are in charge or that circumstances have doomed us. Then we tend to feel either inflated or deflated.

Inflation means feeling special and unique, trying to make special arrangements with destiny. If we accrue such and such amount of wealth, if we do so many good deeds, if we jog or watch our diets, and so on, then bad things shouldn't happen to us. Or perhaps we see ourselves as more talented, intelligent, or important than others. This is also a form of suffering because it sets us apart from the human condition and may prevent us from receiving the gifts that are the birthright of suffering—compassion, wisdom, true creativity. Many people who think of themselves as special hold themselves to impossible conditions and demand long hours of work, or conversely don't work at all because they can never find anything quite worthy of their efforts. I've seen people in psychotherapy who felt that their talents—in writing or painting or performance—were so uniquely special that they could never begin to express them because nothing they could do would bring the desired results (of fame or power or perfection). Consequently, they had not really engaged with anything but had held themselves back—waiting for that "right" moment or relationship that could finally bring their fantasies to fruition.

Deflation is that sense of being completely disabled or depressed—helpless to make life go well, a victim of past traumas or circumstances. Such a person feels automatically left out, never able to measure up to what others have, or seem to have, achieved. A deflated neurotic person will talk incessantly about why she or he cannot do what should or could be done. When solutions are offered by friends or family, they are immediately shown as faulty because the person has "reasons" why the solutions wouldn't work. The implication here is that the person is exempt from the responsibility of returning something to society for the privilege of being alive.

A person in a state of suffering is cut off or alienated from the human circle, feeling left out and different in either a positive (inflated) or negative (deflated) way. This is one kind of misery in human life. The other is the necessary pain of our universal limitations: birth, illness, decay, death, and all of the losses that develop in relation to these.

Can there be freedom from pain and suffering? Not really, because we are all constrained by the same conditions of our bodies, our dependence, and our relationships. The *possibility* of freedom from suffering exists, although most of us will not reach it. More likely, we can achieve a condition in which we reap the benefits of suffering, in which we come to understand how suffering can be alleviated, and how pain can be transformed into compassion and development. Suffering is useful, and not merely a waste of time, when it awakens us to our responsibility for our own attitudes and thoughts and actions. Within suffering are the gifts of self-awareness and compassion.

A PARABLE OF SUFFERING
AND COMPASSION

WE LEARN FROM the resilient how those who acknowledge their suffering can discover knowledge and wisdom and tolerance through helping others. In all of the life stories in this book, helping or wanting to help others is central—it is also a way of helping oneself. Compassion is a suffering-with. It is not sympathy, pity, or simply the urge to do good. Rather, it is a need to help others in order to understand how and why one suffers oneself. And perhaps it is not even that ordered or sequential; it is more of a jumble of one's own suffering or pain and seeing others who are similar and then recognizing oneself within them.

Psychologist and radio talk-show host Dan Gottlieb's life story is a parable of suffering and compassion. Dan's was an ordinary life into which terror, loss, and tragedy came marching. He is no Mother Teresa, nor was he ever. Dan could have been any of us who are trying to be regular and successful—and then an accident resulted in his becoming a quadriplegic. Dan could have wallowed in self-pity for the rest of his life, mucked about in discontent and negativity, and not one of us would have blamed him.

Dan (now age forty-eight) exudes a quiet kind of energy and activity, and works about sixty hours a week doing psychotherapy, teaching, supervising, hosting a national radio talk show, and writing a newspaper column. Although he is bound to a wheelchair and has around-the-clock nurses, I never consider him "disabled" because his life is so active and his engagement with others is so energetic.

Dan Gottlieb grew up in New Jersey with two parents and a sister five years older. "There was a good deal of attention, and I felt loved, but what was missing in my childhood was *empathy*. Like when I didn't make the Babe Ruth Baseball League, just above Little League, I came home crying because it was really important to me. My mother said something like, 'Don't be upset. It's only a game.' My father just echoed her."

Although his father frequently expressed love and admiration for his mother, Dan's mother was "not demonstrative at all" to his father. Dan is unsure whether his mother had real affection for his father, and as he looks back at them now, he thinks they were both depressed. Although he felt loved, he also felt powerless to influence anyone in the family.

Dan's older sister's achievements were valued more than his, and "she was in fact more competent than me in every way." In his younger years, Dan felt out of place at home and out of place at school. He was shorter than average, and his height made him self-conscious. Through all of his growing up and his young adulthood, Dan struggled to feel included, to conform to what was expected for success. By the time he reached his late twenties, Dan felt that he had "made it," that he was recognized as a leader in his field of family therapy and drug and alcohol rehabilitation.

Through his childhood, adolescence, and young adult

years, Dan often felt different from others around him. Although he had explained this feeling to himself as the problem of being "too short," as he looks back now, he believes that this difference was more significant. He believes that he has always felt a deeper connection to life than most people seem to. The first time he witnessed this in himself was in his freshman year in college. "It was 1964 and I had flunked out of my first semester at college. I went to register for the second semester and I wasn't allowed. It was the height of the Vietnam War, and I was terrified that I'd be drafted if I didn't get back into school.

"I called my mother because I didn't know what to do, and she said, 'Look I can't get there to save you this time. You do something about it. Go see the president of the university.' And so I did. I went into his office and brushed past the receptionist who stopped me. She asked me where I thought I was going. I said that I needed to see the president immediately, and she said that I couldn't without an appointment. So I just walked into his office. He was there. I explained my story to him and begged him to let me stay one more semester. He called down to the registrar and told him to let me stay.

"Of course, the word quickly got around the campus administration that this kid had come into the president's office and gotten permission to break the rules. When I got back to the registrar, whose name was Kessler, several people were milling around in his office and he stepped out and said to me, in front of this crowd, 'Gottlieb, you shouldn't be registering, you know you're gonna flunk out.' And everybody looked at me and I said, 'Moses was a prophet, but Kessler's a registrar.' I felt powerful that day."

This first confrontation with the possibility of death (in the Vietnam War) brought an awareness of Dan's responsibility for his own life, as well as the vulnerability of that life. It was Dan's first memorable, major suffering, his first "oh my god, this is really happening to me and I don't want this" experience. He responded to it with a small awakening of self-awareness—the power that comes from responsibility for oneself and the fear that comes with the power. Dan was hardly ready yet to feel responsible, but soon events rushed forward to provoke another confrontation with death.

When Dan was twenty-six, his twenty-three-year-old wife, to whom he had been married for three years, was diagnosed with melanoma. They had two babies, and Dan was deeply scared. "Between the surgery and the chemotherapy, the initial trauma lasted almost eight months. It was one of those shocks that changes you to the core. It was a confrontation with solitude for me, one that I'd never known before. I felt existentially alone, that no one could understand my terror. I was alone facing the death of my partner and best friend, as well as the mother of my very young children."

Dan's wife recovered from her cancer, something for which she and he felt enormously grateful. But the illness and their reactions to it were not all positive. Each did things that hurt the other, and for Dan the entire experience had stirred fears and neuroses that led to greater suffering.

And then Dan's life was irrevocably changed. "At the age of thirty-three, just when I thought I was a pretty powerful guy professionally—running two drug clinics and supervising thirty people and teaching at the Family Institute of

Philadelphia—I encountered the most transformative event of my life. I was driving on the expressway on my way to pick up a Thunderbird to celebrate our tenth wedding anniversary.

"We both had always loved those cars, and I was driving up to meet my Uncle Irv, who was a car dealer near Harrisburg, to get the car. It was December twentieth. I was listening to Donna Summers on my eight-track, feeling really good, a great sunny day. All I remember is seeing a black thing flying through the air. I saw it for a millisecond before it hit me. The truck wheel (from an oncoming tractor-trailer) hit the top of the car and just flattened the car out. People came around and the only thing I remember is saying, 'Call everybody I know and tell them to come here right away.'

"That moment I was a quadriplegic. But I didn't know it for twenty-four hours, although everyone was telling me. It just didn't register. My body was paralyzed and traumatized and so was my mind. I became, in many ways, like an infant, and it would take me eight years to grow up again."

Dan was taken to an intensive care unit at a local hospital in a small Pennsylvania town. Because his neck was broken, his head had to be prevented from moving so there would be no further damage to his spinal cord. Dan and his wife decided that they didn't want the required neurosurgery (a necessity for preventing further injury) to be done at this local hospital, but wanted him transferred to Jefferson Hospital in downtown Philadelphia. However, his condition was considered too unstable to risk transportation.

His wife found out about a piece of equipment called a Halo vest that the local hospital had never heard of. She and

Dan decided to use the vest to secure Dan's head in order for him to make the trip in the ambulance to Philadelphia. "The vest had two parts. There's a headpiece, which is a band of metal about a quarter inch thick that fits around the head. It's literally bolted at four places into your head, from which metal bars come down into a plastic vest that fits around your chest. This is supposed to be put on during surgery while you're under general anesthetic, but they had to put it on me while I was conscious. It was just indescribable pain. They had to use a torque wrench to put the bolts in. I was determined to do it because I felt that going to Jefferson would save my life. It was one of those things where something in me just decided to live and I believed that I had to get to Jefferson in order to live.

"It took us around three hours to get to Philadelphia in the ambulance, and when we arrived, I looked up at the people in the emergency room and said, 'Help me or kill me. Either one is okay.'"

Dan was trying to communicate his level of agony to the staff, but they had little understanding or empathy. Instead of commiserating with him, they sent a psychiatrist to treat him for depression. When the doctor began asking Dan about his relationships in early childhood, Dan demanded that the psychiatrist leave the room.

Most people seemed unable to tolerate seeing Dan bolted into the Halo vest and in such pain. One resident was an exception: "I was very, very, very verbal about my pain and my psychic injury, but no one would listen. Then one young medical resident, walking by the room at about midnight, looked in and saw me and then returned. He just looked at me for a minute or so and said, 'I have no idea what you're going through, but my wife and I just went through a miscarriage, and if your pain is anything like mine, it must be just awful.' I never forgot him."

In this brief interchange, Dan experienced the gift of a stranger's compassion. In directly acknowledging his pain, the resident had reached Dan at the level of some recognizable truth, and for the first time after the accident Dan was open to another person. Unfortunately, though, most people couldn't respond empathically or compassionately to Dan's great pain. For the most part, he felt isolated.

A close personal friend of Dan's "ran away from me." He had visited Dan at the hospital until the first day that Dan was up in a wheelchair, still in the Halo vest. Then the friend just stopped visiting. Much of what they had had in common (like the fun of playing racquetball and talking about their career successes) had now died, and his friend could not stay around so that something else could be born. He couldn't ride his mule backwards or pay enough attention to his own reactions to change them.

When I asked Dan what was helpful and what was hurtful in other people's attempts to help him after the accident, he said that most people were hurtful when they "tried to say helpful things. Like 'I'm glad your arms still partly work.' Or 'Aren't you lucky you still have a career?' A lot of people would tell me how good the future looked and how lucky I was to be alive. Of course, all I wanted to do was die.

"I wanted people to look at me more honestly and say something about the pain. After I got out of the hospital, I was going to a friend's swimming pool with my daughters, who were five and seven at the time. Something happened while we were driving there, maybe I had a bladder accident or something, and my older daughter just blurted out, 'I hate you for ruining my life!' and I felt relieved. I was always so guilty for being a burden, and I knew what she said was true. It helped me feel closer to her. It may sound like a cruel thing to say, but it was actually loving because it was honest and I knew it."

Suffering and pain are transformative when they are faced and expressed in a way that reveals the truth. Dan's daughter went directly into her own suffering and linked it with Dan and his accident and then she spoke straightforwardly. Both she and Dan were suffering from hating Dan, from wishing that life could go back to the past and undo the accident, from wanting to have control where there was no control. Dan benefited from her remark, and so did their relationship, which remains close.

It is the descent into hell—the hell of dukkha, of fantasies and fears—that permits compassion to arise. It is never the sugarcoating, the reassurance, or the mere support, but the real and actual distress that's shared and recognized in compassion. Many myths and stories reveal this symbolically when a god or goddess, prince or princess, willingly sacrifices comfort for pain. This sacrifice is not merely to learn more about oneself, to go "into" the depths of despair in order to see what's there. It is fundamentally about sharing in the limitations of human life and feeling the connection to others through pain and suffering.

Most people were unable to suffer with Dan. They experienced self-consciousness, perhaps their own shame and embarrassment, at seeing him bolted into the vest. They tried to reassure him that "everything will be okay" and that they still loved him. Although Dan could appreciate their love and their self-consciousness, he was not deeply helped by such reassurances, nor had they made any direct connection with him.

But Dan remembers one experience, only about two weeks after the accident, that was uniquely helpful.

"There was a nurse giving out medications one night, and she said to me, 'Is it common to feel suicidal?'—I guess because she knew I was a psychologist—and I said, 'Well, yeah, I think that most people do at some point in their lives, but if you want to talk more, why don't you stop by after your shift?' So at eleven o'clock that night, she came by and we talked for an hour. I don't remember what she said, but I know I referred her to a therapist. That's the first time I knew that I could live as a quadriplegic."

Even before Dan had any notion of what would be required of him to reenter life, he began to recognize that something positive was happening alongside his pain and misery. "I found that some barrier between me and others had disappeared. I remember talking to people in intimate ways in my hospital room, and just floating inside of them and knowing what it was like to be them, and knowing how they felt. A lot of people would come to see me and say that they didn't know why they were coming. It wasn't about their guilt or compulsions or any of that crap. There was something pulling them there and I think it was because of the way I talked and listened to them."

Ultimately, Dan and his wife were not able to keep the

connection between them alive. Dan's wife had been his truest best friend early on after the accident; her devotion to his welfare seemed almost superhuman. But as Dan began to recover some of his functioning and reclaim his strengths (something he might not have done without her help), he felt that she began to pull back. During his stay at a rehabilitation hospital, about six months after the accident, it became clear that she was still aggrieved about some of his responses to her own illness and its aftermath. When Dan finished the initial round of his rehabilitation and began to reclaim his career, he and his wife grew further apart. Ten years after Dan's accident, they separated and eventually divorced.

Feeling a deep parental bond with his daughters, Dan eliminated the "option for suicide" after his accident and decided to get on with life, although he was frequently overcome with shame, resentment, and self-pity. "I still saw myself as the old Dan who was incompetent when it came to holding a pencil or a fork or putting on a jacket, these simple things. Every time I went by a golf course or a baseball field or saw people dancing, it was like being faced with my death. I just heard a voice saying over and over, 'You'll never do these things again.'

"I was terribly dependent and ashamed of it for the first two years. I was ashamed that I needed help peeing and cutting my food. I was ashamed of the emotional dependence, too. The shame was excruciating, but I began to see that it was optional. So I turned things inside out and began to talk about my dependence and my shame, to address men especially and say how much strength is required to talk about your weakness. It's an act of courage, an act of faith. The old Dan began to die, as I saw that I could help others face their shame and dependence. But it didn't feel like heroism. It felt more like cowardice."

Talking openly and deeply about his weaknesses is a strength of Dan's compassion as he repeatedly transforms his own pain and suffering into comfort and knowledge for others who are suffering. *Turning things inside out* means paying attention to your own reactions and seeing what kind of reality you are creating. When Dan began to talk about his own responses—his shame about dependence—he was suffering with others, putting his difficulties into words not to complain about them but to join with other people with similar problems, to say that they were not alone.

When I asked whether he thought that suffering would continue beyond death, Dan responded, "I don't want suffering to go on for one more minute. My suffering has brought me gifts, but it's really terribly painful too, and at this stage of my life, I'd rather dance than be any wiser."

He doesn't pretend for a minute that his life is easy. In Dan's honesty about how extraordinary his pain and suffering have been, we recognize that we also have a choice about our own reactions to our lives, that we can be victims or we can be free to engage within our limitations.

Dan often mentions how he is different from most people he knows: he has embraced life again and again, whether it has meant staying out of Vietnam (which meant death to him), being an involved parent while financially supporting his ex-wife, or leading an active life as a quadriplegic. "I have always clutched onto life so hard and fought so hard to stay alive that I think when they close my casket, they'll have to pull my hands away from grasping the lid."

Dan says that he is personally unafraid of death, but he is acutely aware of how terrified most people become when they enter into terminal illness. He has seen terminally ill people in therapy. For himself, having faced death repeatedly and in a variety of ways, "I think I'm more afraid of my wheelchair breaking down than of dying.

"When I think of living and dying, everything falls into order. It's like I have my context. In my life, maybe in most, death has to be the context. I know all the time that my life is fragile. This might be my last winter, my last spring. I feel such a pressure to live fully, knowing it might be the end. If there's a sunny day this winter, I want to be in the sun because there may never be another sunny day in the winter for me. There might not be another day at all."

I titled the story of Dan's life a "parable" of suffering and compassion because his life teaches us specifically about suffering—the dissatisfaction and alienation that arise from wanting things to be different from how they are—and compassion. Dan has had to accept and tolerate enormous pain, loss, and misery of all sorts, but he has transformed the suffering that accompanies his pain into his purpose in life. By opening up to others his own reactions to his pain, Dan has reached countless people through his national radio show "Voices in the Family" at WHYY in Philadelphia, helping them to see that they are not alone in feeling ashamed, dependent, afraid, and angry. In their connection to him, they begin to be hopeful about making their lives and relationships work. "My suffering and my injuries have brought something to the fore that's of value to others. And that I truly feel is my purpose in life. I make others less afraid, first of me and then of themselves. In the same way I had to go through the process of becoming less afraid of me, of my own dependency and vulnerability, of my own death and my nakedness, I show others how to be less afraid."

I asked Dan directly what he thought might be at the core of his resilience, what the most important factors were. "We can talk about my own history and my genes, and that's a piece of it, but the biggest piece is having a purpose. My career on the radio has carried me through; it's a large part of what saved my life. The show came to me before I had a so-called spiritual awakening, but when it was offered I felt like it was God saying, 'Okay, I broke your neck, but now you can have this in exchange.'" The show has led to thousands of relationships that Dan has developed with people "who don't have bodies—kind of like me" and who listen to him faithfully. A belief in purpose transcends all of the ongoing pain. He deeply believes that he might never have found a purpose had he not broken his neck.

But Dan is practical also, and he reminds me that "economics contributed to my resilience. My insurance policy—no-fault insurance—bought me my wheelchair, modified my house, and bought me my wheelchair van. It's paid about four million dollars so far. You might think it's mundane, but if I didn't have insurance, I might be on welfare or homeless or whatever, and I don't think I'd have much resilience then."

So economics also enters into this story of suffering and compassion. Circumstances surrounding a person's life obviously have major effects on how painful any trauma or accident will be. And yet the degree of suffering—the degree of discontent or off-centeredness—is always affected primarily by the meaning made of the events, the reactions and responses that we bring.

Compassion, the knowledge that comes from suffering with others, is a tremendous gift. It comes from deeply and truthfully recognizing your own suffering and pain, valuing it for its truth, its thereness. Anyone reading this book can grasp the usefulness of suffering in awakening us to our own reactions and to our potential to be compassionate. But to take the first step of transformation—from recognition to compassion—requires more than mere motivation.

The descent into hell begins with being authentic about pain and difficulties, opening them up and facing them directly. But it proceeds quickly into suffering—into seeing how one creates for oneself many of the problems that are troubling. The challenge of unpacking one's suffering is no small issue all along the way. But to unpack our suffering is to awaken to self-knowledge, an understanding of who we are, that cannot be reached in any other way.

Mapping Our Personal
Complexes

Suffering has great value because it is a signal that we should pay attention to our reactions, the assumptions we're bringing to experience. To deny, cover up, or run away from suffering is useless and harmful, and yet it is understandable. When people enter psychotherapy, or when they seek help from educators and theologians, from family and friends, and from books like this, they are often suffering as much as or more than they are feeling pain. To recognize suffering and be willing to express the recognition is the first step toward transformation.

What we see among the resilient, among those who transform their suffering into growth and development, is always that *first* willingness to recognize and express their pain, as when Dan was very verbal about the pain and suffering of wearing the Halo vest.

Before quelling suffering with prescription or nonprescription drugs, we would do well to enter its terrain and walk around a bit. If we dismiss it as "dysfunctional"—as though the term had magic to absolve our own complicity in our difficulties—then we won't be interested in what we can learn from it.

If we take a perspective of responsibility and interest—in both the pain and the suffering—and hold the tension of wanting to resolve it too quickly, we can begin to map the patterns that underlie our responses. What are the ideals, wishes, fears, and demands we put on ourselves? Where do they come from? Who are they connected with from the past? Why do we cling to them?

After beginning to map the wishes, fears, or obsessions that give personal form and meaning to our suffering, we may feel better prepared to take the next step—to help others who are also in pain or suffering, and that includes absolutely everyone.

Giving help and developing compassion will ease and eradicate the self-consciousness and negativity of dukkha that keep us bound to shame, envy, guilt, or embarrassment—the emotions that fuel the sense of alienation, of being victimized, that always accompanies suffering, no matter how great or trivial its cause. As we'll see later in this book, the self-conscious emotions (from shame to pride) feed our feelings that we are separate little selves housed in separate bodies, somehow fundamentally unique and different from one another. Separateness is reinforced by beliefs that we should protect ourselves, that what we might "give" to another will be "taken" from the self.

Feelings of defensive separateness—some kind of fantasied "independence"—are where many of us are deeply stuck in suffering. Whether the self is felt as a nation, a race, a gender, a group, a family, or a body, if it is seen primarily as isolated and independent, suffering and destruction will ensue from its life—and alienation will permeate its existence.

Often the experience of helping others, as for Dan, is the first step out of the confusion of negativity, self-protection, and destructiveness. Many people are not prepared to help, though, because they are too encased in self-consciousness and fears. The best they can offer others is a "cheer up" kind of assistance that often hurts more than helps. Many of us may have to examine our suffering and learn about our own psychological complexes (the ways we re-create difficult situations) before we can be truly compassionate.

Suffering is frequently hard to claim, and even harder to encounter directly, because we are often completely unconscious of how we're creating it and why it arises. When people are caught in a pattern of unconscious motivations, they typically feel that they are being true to their feelings, even if these are extreme, and that they have little choice about what they are doing.

I don't know what the conditions were that resulted in the difficulties that finally ended Dan's marriage, a relationship and friendship that at first seemed strengthened after his accident. But often in such situations, both partners are engaged in "psychological complexes." Jung used this term (which originally came from one of his teachers, Pierre Janet) to name a phenomenon that he and others had observed many times in patients and other people. A complex is an unconscious drama, usually with roles for self and others, that is played out by its author with flair and absolute belief in its truth or grounding, although it may look to others to be complete irrationality.

Every complex contains unconscious behaviors and beliefs. When people observe someone else "in a complex," they see someone reacting with strong emotions, seemingly completely convinced of the validity of the actions, and moving on the basis of impulse from one set of assumptions to another, almost relentlessly.

Every complex is grounded in a particular set of images and meanings marked by emotions. For example, most of us have some kind of Great Mother complex that is enacted or sought in regard to strong nurturance (the desire to give or receive it) and comforting feelings and images. This came into being through nurturance in our early relationships, the ways in which our tensions were eased and our needs responded to. Back then, in earliest childhood, we didn't know the category "woman," but later when we understood that category, we may have assigned our expectations for nurturance to a woman, usually the one we call Mother. Later that same Great Mother complex may be brought to bear on a love relationship in which we expect nurturance, attention, and idealization like those we felt we got from Mom.

If our nurturing experiences were mostly negative, or more mixed and ambivalent, then we also have a Terrible Mother complex that may exist alongside the Great Mother. The Terrible Mother complex involves the images, tastes, sounds, smells, and handling that were painful, disruptive, unattuned, and nonempathic. If we developed both positive and negative mother complexes (which most of us have), then we sometimes saw Mother as a goddess and sometimes as a witch. These images were rooted in our own emotional states more than specifically in what Mother might be saying or doing. She would provoke some reaction in us, but the provocation might be small while the reaction would be large.

A mass of past experiences held together by an emotional core, a psychological complex has a life of its own outside of our conscious intentions. It can strongly influence our personal style and behaviors and be fully out of awareness. When activated, it puts us into a "mood" that we cannot seem to shake. People may feel or say "I'm really beside myself" when they're in a complex, and others will agree.

When a complex—whether ideal or negative—is activated, we may identify with it or project it into another person. By projection I mean that we "see" it or experience it as being activated by or belonging to someone else, often a partner or a child or parent. We may do both, interweaving identification and projection. Dan may have felt he was the victim child of a negative parental complex when his wife did things that were hurtful to him. He may have felt that it was "all her fault" and that she "caused" the situation that led to her actions. But Dan may also have reacted as a negative parent, withdrawing and criticizing and not sustaining contact. Even though he felt like the victim, he might have sounded or acted like the aggressor.

We could also say that Dan probably formed an inferiority complex in regard to his sister and his mother. He felt unable to match his sister's skills and competencies, and felt that his mother rarely praised him for any of his own (while seeming to prefer his sister's strengths). Dan felt ashamed, rejected, jealous, and envious. As he grew older and moved more into the world (before his accident), he felt he obtained "proof" that his mother was right in finding him inferior because he believed he was "too short" to fit in socially, and that he wasn't "smart enough." This complex may have been activated again with his wife or other women—with whom he might have competed but felt inferior (as with his sister) or believed he disappointed and could never satisfy (as he felt about his mother).

A person captured by a complex seems almost to be in a hypnotic trance. There is a sense of being swept away by one's emotions and reactions; often people say they're "responding from the gut" and tend to believe that this is the truest depth of their feelings. Even when someone is alternately acting like a victim child and an angry terrible parent, she or he is unlikely to see the inconsistencies that another might point out. It all just seems true and necessary to the person enacting the complex.

No one escapes being shaped by complexes, because they are the structures of personality. By the time we reach adulthood, we're all driven by some powerful complexes that originated in our experiences in primary relationships—self, mother, father, sister, brother—and are then woven seamlessly into the rational explanations we give to the meaning of our existence. Even the most emotionally driven people, those who are labeled "psychotic," have "rational" explanations for the distorted images they defend as being true. We all try to make our emotional realities fit what we come to know of the world around us and to find explanations that we think others are likely to accept.

At the core of every complex is an archetype, a universal tendency to form a coherent image in a highly aroused emotional state. We all have images of Terrible Mothers (witches, nags, hags, stepmothers) and Great Mothers (goddesses, nurturers, comforters), Terrible Fathers (demons and devils), Great Fathers (gods and kings), Divine Children, and

Magicians. Negative and positive complexes form around the archetypes of human psychological experiences and are carried forth into our expectations and assumptions about the world and reality.

We could say, as Jung did, that our psychological complexes become the *karma* we bring with us from our earliest days, our experiences of family and caregivers. I'll discuss karma, a Buddhist term, in greater detail later. This Sanskrit word literally means "action" and refers to the fact that we are affected directly by the consequences of our own intentions and actions. Our attitudes and actions lead to much of what simply appears to "happen to us." The Buddhist scholar Gunapala Dharmasiri has suggested that "The Buddhist theory of karma can be best explained in terms of C. G. Jung's theory of complexes." Contrary to what many Westerners believe, the Buddhist notion of karma is not of predetermination, but of the fluid development from moment to moment of certain consequences from our own attitudes and actions.

We are each born into a family constellation at a particular moment in time. A great drama is already under way in that family, something that has strong emotional pulls made up in large part from the roles of the parents (and their parents before and so on) and, in lesser part, from the siblings. Dan was born two years after a first child, his sister, who would always be cherished for her intelligence and verbal skills. Dan's own temperament and emotional attitudes played important parts in his forming an inferiority complex, but some ingredients were already present.

Psychological complexes are not the same thing as "family

history" or a "family system." Every family member has different complexes of mother, father, sister, and brother because each member has been drawn in and responded in unique emotional ways to the conditions and situations of the original family.

But the family history or system has its own particular relational patterns and attitudes that stretch back over the generations, repeating certain possibilities and certain barriers. These are also family karma, the motives and assumptions and the schemes and ideals, into which the new child will be woven. Even from the time of its conception, the child is the object of fantasy and speculation as well, taking a place (conscious or unconscious) in the parents' imaginations. In no way is a child a blank slate, waiting to be written on by life.

As we come to know more about karma over the course of this book, we'll see how subtle its implications are. From Buddhism we learn that we create many of the conditions of our lives through our assumptions, expectations, and impulses, as well as our direct actions. These conditions lead to people responding to us in ways that may be difficult or supportive, that can cause us pain or bring us satisfaction. Jung's theory of psychological complexes comes very close to mirroring the Buddhist theory of karma, at least in regard to showing us how we have strong emotional tendencies to create and re-create the themes and images that we were born into, especially situations that were disappointing or left us desiring more. Where there have been strong emotional patterns in childhood, there will be strong tendencies to create the same patterns in adulthood. Often the more painful and distressing themes will be the most powerful as people unconsciously try to complete, cure, or heal those family members (as we imagine them) who seemed to be the most ill, afraid, or weak. Generally speaking, human beings cannot let go of the emotional deprivations and wounds of the past until they can become aware of what they are, and what they mean. If you were born to parents who were afraid, depressed, and life-denying, or to ones who were secure, confident, and life-affirming, you will tend to replay the major emotional themes of childhood in later relationships *until* you become aware of what you are doing, with enough objective understanding in order to change your point of view. Of course, you do not replay these scenes from some "realistic" or objective point of view; you create them as you knew them, as you experienced them, with all of your own prejudices and fantasies built in. Karma is the "law" of human nature that says there will be consequences of our own attitudes and actions that will carry through to shape the reality of our lives. Our complexes are illustrations of how our attitudes and actions create and re-create certain realities.

There is a coherence between our expectations and actions and the karma (complex) that shapes them:

> A karma always attains fruition in a way that is similar to the original act performed . . .

In other words, some of our miseries—those connected with our personal suffering—are specifically related to us. They are the consequences of our own wishes, actions, intentions, and the ways in which we have unconsciously enacted or disclaimed them. If we seem caught in a dance of destruction and negativity, it is a dance that we're doing, a show that we're sponsoring. Dan grew to understand that his shame (about his losses and dependence) was rooted in early patterns of shame, and that he did not need to continue to re-create the same feelings of not fitting in. Of course, he fully realized this only *after* he broke his neck, after his body was so different from what he wanted and so generally unlike others that he could have drowned in his shame. Instead, Dan's suffering became an opportunity for development, the first step of which was made with those first few experiences of compassion—the resident who linked his own pain to Dan's; the nurse who asked for help with suicidal impulses; Dan's daughter's deeply felt "I hate you" statement, spoken out of her love and need. These were among the moments that sustained him through long periods of alienation, shame, and fear during the eight years that were his road back to a fully engaged life.

Sometimes, though, the direct experience of authentic pain can propel one completely beyond old neurotic habits, as I've seen in a few people who have encountered serious illness, betrayal, or loss unexpectedly. They were suddenly able to move beyond their neurotic quirks to become compassionate.

To engage in compassion relieves suffering and makes pain tolerable. Here is an account from a courageous young woman who struggled against breast cancer for four years and finally died, thoroughly healed through her experiences along the way. Treya Wilber, the wife and partner of the philosopher Ken Wilber, recorded her responses to the failures of and confusion about late-stage chemotherapy for an advanced, recurring cancer:

> I felt incredibly shaky, crying a lot, very agitated, close to falling apart, dwelling on fears of pain and thoughts of death . . . and then would come thoughts of all who are suffering on this planet at this moment, of all who have suffered in the past, and I would immediately feel a wave of peace and calm pass through me. I no longer felt alone. I no longer felt singled out; instead I felt an incredible connection with all these people, like we were part of the same huge family.

In her mind's eye, she saw children who die of cancer, people who are killed suddenly in accidents, parents who endure the death of a child, thousands of people who die in war and of starvation. She was no longer alone, no longer separated out and victimized. True compassion is a powerful antidote to our own suffering because it counteracts alienation.

In learning the freedom and wisdom of suffering-with, the resilient discover a new, bigger context in which their lives make sense. This context always has some essential connection to the larger questions about our existence, about life and death, and brings immediate awareness of the ways in which all living beings are joined through their dependence on each other. This is where deep and true creativity is born, outside the boundaries of self-consciousness and negativity and within a strong focus on love and connection.

To stay relatively free of suffering is to stay very awake

and conscious of our tendencies to create it. They may never disappear, although they will weaken. What seems to work best in holding onto this awareness is some kind of practice or belief that returns you again and again to compassion and connection with others. This produces a different kind of attitude about pain, loss, and even death. It is a deep belief that life's experiences cannot be overwhelming, defeating, or disintegrating because they will all move toward greater integration when held in the proper framework.

In Part Three, I will discuss people who discover the knowledge of compassion even in childhood, who find the gifts of suffering as a first step in a lifetime of purpose and meaning.

Some Advantages of a Difficult Childhood

Difficulty at the beginning works supreme success,
Furthering through perseverance.
    The I Ching OR Book of Changes

SOME OF US who encountered adversity in childhood have embraced it as a daemon of creative insight and purpose and lived fully, without too much envy or resentment. Others have become magnets for attracting more pain, always susceptible to re-creating what hurt them. The difference seems to lie in the attitude taken toward suffering and pain. Some people learn early to ride the mule backwards and to see value in their losses and difficulties, a value that connects them to a purpose in life.

Part Three explores the characteristics of resilience from childhood adversity—trauma, loss, and conflict. It may speak to you directly or indirectly. If you had a difficult childhood, but tend to dismiss your strengths or abilities (at least in part) because you doubt their validity, you are likely to find your strengths directly reflected in these pages. You'll find a deepened appreciation for the gains that can accompany childhood adversity.

Some popular psychology, especially the kind that labels families as "dysfunctional," can mislead people into thinking that a difficult childhood is nothing more than a liability to be overcome through medications or affirmations. It formalizes, in oversimplified labels of blame (other-blame or self-blame), the complex issues of loving a parent ambivalently or responding usefully to a parent's unfair needs. What is lost in the process is any belief or understanding of the transformative power of pain and the benefits that can accrue from early knowledge of how to be emotionally helpful to others who are more vulnerable, even if they happen to be your parents.

Those of you who haven't experienced a difficult childhood will find a more indirect message here: there's a "natural" path from adversity to greater meaning, and it has been discovered even by children. This path, like the one in fairy tales that brings vulnerable children safely home after meeting witches or demons, is archetypal. In Buddhism it is reflected in the Noble Truths that describe what is required to ease our own and others' suffering. We find these truths illustrated in the story I told earlier of the Zen master and the samurai who wanted to know about heaven and hell. When provoked by life's difficulties, if we can keep calm and reflective and see the situation in a bigger context, then we can find heaven—even in the midst of chaos. But if we respond to fear with aggression or to danger with collapse, then we are opening the gates to hell.

Those resilient from childhood adversity are extraordinary

models of how to thrive after overwhelming odds. They are not simply survivors. They achieve prosperity, stable home lives, and rich relationships, and possess a strong sense of purpose. When I first read studies of the resilient, I was both shocked by the ugliness and pain of their abuses, traumas, and losses, and inspired by their resilience.

Their resilience showed that childhood difficulties could bring advantages, and there are specific studies of how this occurs. This knowledge became the background music for my work in therapy. In addition to helping people recognize their own complexes and take responsibility for the suffering they created, I began to look for what seemed natural to the resilient: the process by which we all can transform our difficulties into discovery and development, making use of our own miseries to find a purpose in life.

Twenty-five years ago, most psychologists—especially developmental psychologists and psychoanalysts—would have thought it folly to believe that a traumatic childhood could produce a fully functioning adult. The prevailing wisdom was that although such a person might look good on the surface, be successful in business or creative work, she or he was miserable underneath, probably making others miserable as well. The thought then was that the losses of childhood are irretrievable, and although we might compensate for them, they can never really be transformed into health and inspiration—especially into fully functioning relationships. Relational wounds from childhood were thought to leave irremediable scars that would always produce poor relational skills later.

We now know that this isn't so. Some children have

transformed the pain of their difficult childhoods into gifts that have lasted a lifetime. The early death of a parent, leading to abandonment depression and fears, can become an ability to express loss in poetry, fiction, or painting. Narcissistic wounds from parenting that lacked empathy and warmth can be transformed into service to children who have been wounded by abuse and neglect. Or, as in my case, early witnessing of family discord can lead to a keen ability to unpack and understand what drives people to hurt one another, which resulted in my career as a psychoanalyst.

We know now from longitudinal studies that approximately one in ten people who grew up in difficult conditions—with the strain of poverty, discord, loss, or parents' mental illness—is exceptionally competent as an adult. Sometimes these unusual individuals have been dubbed invulnerable or invincible, but we now realize that that label is misleading. No one is invulnerable. It is the way that vulnerability is faced, examined, and treated that leads to resilience.

Although most children of adversity and trauma do not have the resources of those 10 percent, research shows that many lead effective lives. What protects some people from later entanglements after having been abused or traumatized, while others re-create their childhood suffering in their adult lives? The common ingredients in struggling against loss, pain, and cruelty are help, hope, and meaning.

People who study the resilient are developing a philosophy about promoting resilience in all of us. The most favorable beginning in life for later resilience "may not be a life without adversity, but rather a life with graduated challenges that enhance the development of mastery skills, flexible coping strategies, and adaptive personality attributes," say two well-known researchers. This philosophy of graduated challenges can inspire all of us to encounter adversity with an eye toward what it teaches, at any stage of life. It is never too late to learn from the resilient.

WHAT PROTECTS THE
RESILIENT?

ALTHOUGH A FEW highly resilient individuals seem able to convert overwhelming odds into graduated challenges, most of us would find severe childhood adversity too difficult to integrate while we continue to grow. But even if we're not able to identify with the strengths of the resilient, we can learn from their experience that responsibility and a larger context of meaning (larger than self-pity, for instance) lead to greater self-determination and even self-confidence.

The social and environmental activist Joanna Macy appreciates the adversity and pain she felt in childhood, without complaint that she did not have a secure, happy one: "Only humans can suffer in the way we do and only humans can change their karma." She means that the difficult conditions endured as a part of childhood, conditions into which we're born, can be remedied and changed through our own awareness and development. Anyone who truly transcends the suffering of a difficult childhood, and works to change the world in ways that improve it, has reversed a fundamental bit of adversity, has turned her or his life around and has much to teach us all.

The psychiatrist Michael Rutter, eminent researcher of resilience, is firmly convinced that the strengths of the resilient are more than constitutional factors, such as genetic advantages or good temperament. He stresses their active engagement and responses to their life situation. "We need to ask why and how some individuals manage to maintain high self-esteem and self-efficacy in spite of facing the same adversities that lead other people to give up and lose hope."

Rutter's pioneering studies led psychologists to reassess the issues of childhood adversity. He has developed a list of six major childhood stressors that are highly associated with risk for later emotional disorders. These were not drawn from psychotherapy but were collected in a longitudinal study of people living on the Isle of Wight in England.

The study, which followed people from childhood into middle adulthood, identified the most common risk factors that can lead to later psychological difficulties:

> severe marital discord
> low social status of the family
> overcrowding or large family size
> criminality of the father
> psychiatric disorder of the mother
> admitting the child into care of local authorities.

Any of the above might be combined with any of the others, and often include additional symptoms of chaotic family life, such as physical and sexual abuse of children.

What Protects the Resilient?

The resilient react to childhood stresses, even severe ones, differently from their less resilient counterparts. They teach us about renewal and transformation, but people less successful—sometimes dubbed the vulnerable—teach us about the susceptibility to deterioration under continuing stress.

This kind of vulnerability is frequently rooted in the negative evaluation of oneself or life's circumstances. When life's pressures mount, we are susceptible to turning stress into ongoing difficulty: an illness, a neurosis, an addiction, a destructive pattern of relationships.

Even for the resilient, vulnerability to new stress is always present. When I asked Joanna if she thought her childhood adversity had created any barriers in her development, she said: "I've been chronically susceptible to illness all my life. I'd be surprised if these things weren't related to the experience of so much fear over so long. Also I've had problems with my anger—too much intensity in my feelings, just like my father. It hasn't been easy for me to relax, but I'm getting better at it in my sixties now. I've always had that haunting feeling that the trap door's going to fall, that something is going to do me in." Joanna is describing the roots of her own psychological complexes. On one end of the spectrum is a Terrible Father complex of intense anger and a desire to control things. And on the other is a feeling of being a victim of chance circumstances (that sense of powerlessness that is the mark of childhood complexes), just as she had felt when faced with her father's unpredictable rages.

How much are people in general at risk for severe psychological complexes, for ongoing suffering and vulnerability in adult life? You've probably read the incredible statistics on sexual and physical abuse of children. You may know that the divorce rate is about 50 percent for first-marrieds and over 60 percent for remarried couples. So you would probably guess that many people are at risk for later suffering from a difficult childhood. But perhaps you'll be surprised, as I was, to learn that a large majority in our society have endured major trauma or abuse in their childhood.

Two large surveys of college students asked questions about childhood experiences of highly stressful events, such as divorce, severe marital conflict, and serious illness in oneself or a family member. Both surveys reported a *majority* of students experiencing such events by the age of eighteen. One survey, by Lauterbach and Vrana, found that only 17 percent said they had not experienced a highly stressful event. From this information on college students, we can estimate with certainty a comparable or worse situation for those people who have not attended college. Overall, then, when we think about who is at risk for later suffering from childhood trauma, we're talking about *most* of us, not some small group.

The social-work researcher Leavelle Cox has summarized some of the personality features that appear to be characteristic of the resilient, drawing especially on the psychoanalytic theory of Heinz Kohut. Her list matches what I think will eventually emerge from research now being done. She (and I) would bet that the following are some of the major characteristics that would predict resilience:

the ability and wish to feel and understand the needs of others

the ability to compromise and to delay meeting one's own
desires in order to meet the needs of others

the potential for creative development

humor—being able to laugh good-naturedly at one's previous mistakes or fanaticisms

wisdom—coming to grips with the meaning of one's life
and one's limitations

These personality traits would predict resilience whether it
occurs in response to a sudden illness or loss, in response to
a childhood of misery, or in response to social or environmental catastrophe. My four friends whose life stories are
told throughout this book exhibit great empathy, flexibility,
creativity, humor, and wisdom.

HELP

THE RESILIENT LEARN early how to help. Knowing that one is helpful to others appears to strengthen rather than deplete a developing self. Those who can later engage their suffering creatively often report that it was more the love they *gave* than the love they *received* that saved them from despair.

Joanna Macy is uncertain whether she'll be able to grasp in this lifetime the full significance of growing up with her father. From the beginning of his marriage, he blamed her mother for spending money, for needing too much for rent and other necessities. He was occasionally physically violent, but mostly it was "tongue lashings which were extraordinarily hurtful. He was powerfully eloquent and used this against my mother and me. It was like getting an electric shock that turns your brain to jelly."

Young Joanna offered support for her mother. "I was trying to defend her from him. When I spoke up, I had nobody backing me.

"I got clobbered. My mother—I was trying to keep her from killing herself—never defended me. I was about nine years old or so when it got to be terrible. She left my father when I was nineteen, but during those ten years, it was awful. I consciously made the decision to save her life when I was nine." Although her mother overconfided in her, Joanna also felt she was loving and affirming, leaving Joanna vehemently on her mother's side in marital disputes. For the ten years until her parents separated, Joanna was the only person fighting her father. She fought him with words—confronting and talking back—and she was unwilling to be silenced.

Although Joanna recognizes that her mother may have leaned too much on her, she also sees her early protection of her mother as linked to the abiding concerns of her later life. "The difficulty of beholding injustice and terror, my mother's terror: witnessing it became a theme over my lifetime. In my twenties it was the civil rights movement. What I saw Papa do was intolerable and what I saw the Klan do was intolerable. So I find myself moving into the last decade of the twentieth century confronting issues of denial, denial of oppression, denial of people's needs, and of the nuclear and environmental dangers we've created."

Joanna is the author of five books widely known for integrating the teachings of Buddhism with social responsibility and activism. She has a distinct gift for seeing what is hidden and revealing its meaning through her perceptions. At this time she is speaking out about the dangers of nuclear waste. In workshops and conferences in many countries, she has helped others look into their own despair and face fears about the future. As she looks back, now in her sixties, Joanna realizes that she found her strong voice in childhood.

She believes that she was provided early in life with the voice and the energy to do the work she does now. In a group exercise that Joanna conducts at national workshops on Despair and Empowerment, she asks people to imagine that they have chosen to be born at this particular moment in history, when human beings have discovered nuclear power and weapons. "We must come to terms finally with our own destructiveness. You decide to be born now because we're going to need all the wits, smarts, compassion, and wisdom that can be mustered. You get to choose your parents. Who would you pick, knowing that whoever you choose, they must prepare you for this mix of joy and destruction that life now contains?"

The idea of choosing our parents comes from Buddhism and is related to the notion that we're drawn into this life through particular needs and desires that carry over from an earlier lifetime. And so we're attracted to particular people as our parents.

Whether or not you find this belief congenial, Joanna has found that the idea of choosing one's parents has brought greater acceptance of her own parents. She says, "I believe I'd choose my same parents again because I can see how they induced the character and attitudes I have, preparing me for the work I feel called to do." Even though her father terrified and tyrannized everyone at home and her mother took little responsibility for the situation, Joanna's parents provided her with her greatest gifts: her intensity and determination to uncover what is really going on in a situation of fear or danger, and her emphatic desire to help others.

The psychologist Gina O'Connell Higgins (herself a resilient adult) conducted in-depth interviews with forty adults who had endured terrifying, cruel childhood experiences, and who now see themselves and are described by others as being highly successful in work *and* love. In midlife, they were chosen for her study especially because of their capacities to love well.

She found that the participants in her study recognized the value of love and compassion, even while they were being abused as children. Most were able to carry over their capacities into making loving families in their adult lives. A woman named Shibvon, a forty-year-old pediatric nurse, has been married to the same man for more than twenty years in a warm, close relationship. Together they have parented three sons.

Shibvon's nursing specialty is caring for infants in an intensive care unit in an urban setting; she is well known for her empathy, especially in a crisis. She sees her career as having begun at age seven, maybe younger, when she tried to nourish her younger siblings in the midst of overwhelming brutality and attacks. She remembers a horrible day when, during a family picnic, she and her five-year-old brother were suddenly taken by the police into protective custody.

Because it was an emergency pickup, the two children had to spend the night in the police station, where they could clearly hear adults around them saying, "What are we going to do with *them?*" Shibvon recalls how important it was to her, at seven, to act mature and not cry so that her brother wouldn't be afraid.

We might think that Shibvon's holding back tears would be harmful to her in a situation of such great fear and confusion, but it was the *meaning* of her action and not the action itself that was important. Helping someone more vulnerable than herself was the context of Shibvon's memory of the event. She didn't see the occasion as one in which she was denied her own expression (or the right to "be a child"), but she saw it more as her first "assignment" in nursing, to protect her little brother from feeling too afraid.

Life for young Shibvon only grew worse after she and her brother returned home from an orphanage where they had stayed for about a year. Her mother's boyfriend repeatedly sexually abused Shibvon, with the mother's obvious assent. Ashamed and in chronic pain from anal intrusions, Shibvon constantly had to leave her classes at school to sit on the toilet in the girls' bathroom. She comforted herself "with a fierce belief that her inescapable ordeal" preserved "her younger siblings from similar intrusions." Although alone in the ordeal, Shibvon linked her trauma to the idea of helping others, and then she found she could endure it. She recalls feeling content that her younger siblings were growing up safely, outside the grip of sexual abuse. Shibvon's resilience was the product not of her cruel abuse—something that still disgusts her—but of finding a meaning within it. Her intention to help her siblings allowed her to continue to believe in the power of love even in the moment of abuse.

In a study of children who were reared by emotionally ill parents in conditions of poverty, researchers identified twenty-five who seemed to be resilient in adolescence. They were more intelligent, pleasing, and curious than their less resilient peers, but more surprising was that every one of them seemed to fulfill a need in one or both of their emotionally ill parents. There was a good match between the child's abilities and a clear need of a parent. The experience of being helpful contributed to a positive self-image and confidence in the child.

The picture of children caring for mentally ill parents, of young Shibvon containing her own fear in order to help her siblings, or of nine-year-old Joanna Macy devoting herself to saving her mother seems to go against the general therapeutic wisdom that early, unfair demands on children will produce lasting damage to the child's developing self. By and large, the general wisdom is true. But there are exceptions as we've discovered from studies of resilience. If abused children were convinced that their pain was useful, especially in helping others, then they were more likely to be resilient.

The psychologist Manfred Bleuler did research on children who grew up with schizophrenic parents. He discovered that living with a mentally ill parent can be manageable—even enhancing—when the children are able to develop skills to care for their parents and to protect themselves from being confused or misled by the parents' illness. When children learned to discriminate what is crazy from what is not, and how to help their parents stay emotionally calm, the children benefited. Bleuler says that the resilient in his study learned from the "therapy of helping others." Knowing that you've actually helped an ill parent or sibling as a child is, according to Bleuler, an indication that you can "fulfill a great task."

Joanna Macy felt, as many resilient adults do, that her own transformation began right in the middle of her terror. "I just kept trying to make do. I wasn't going to lie down and die. I was going to have a life and achieve and help others."

Fifteen resilient African American adults, interviewed by

the social-work researcher Leavelle Cox, had grown up in an atmosphere of family violence—including fights, bloodshed, the use of weapons between parents—but none had been abusive as adults. They talked of assuming responsibility early, even as early as age four or five, and working hard to help the family. Caring for the home, nurturing younger siblings, managing and budgeting money, and working on a farm were some of the ways they helped in childhood. This kind of responsibility was rarely deemed a burden as these adults looked back. Indeed, most of them believed that such responsibility allowed them to be self-determining and that the help they were able to provide to others gave them an early feeling of self-confidence.

The Zen master and teacher Philip Kapleau describes something similar: "When I was fifteen, I got interested in the problem of my mother resenting my younger brother. She was forty-seven when she had him and she detested my father." Because the family was poor and often on welfare, Kapleau worked from an early age. He looks back on his early responsibility, and his emotional distress at his brother's humiliation, as his first step toward Buddhism. He felt compassion for his brother then. Later he felt compassion for his mother's predicament as well. Feeling responsible for himself led to an early sense of autonomy in Kapleau.

Because Joanna Macy understood so little of what was behind her father's violent temper, I wondered if it was hard for her to find compassion for him. She responded that her experience in working with other wounded parents and children has helped her fundamentally to forgive her father. "I've come a long way in my life, and although I can't understand precisely what went wrong for my father in his childhood,

I have almost a diagnostic intuition of what it was like for him as an adult and I feel sad about it. Even as a child, I could tell that there was something wrong with him, that he wasn't normal."

WHAT ABOUT THE HELP the resilient receive? Is it transformative or focal for their later lives? What is surprising in their stories is how little help most had. For some, like Joanna Macy, there was one caring parent or grandparent or older sibling in the immediate surrounding. But for many others, like Shibvon, who remembers only one young teacher who briefly treated Shibvon with sympathetic concern, there were only momentary connections with people who seemed to recognize the risk and vulnerability in the child's life.

For many resilient children, the helpers are far outside of the troubled families. They are teachers or pastors or community leaders who, often for only a brief moment and sometimes just once, show or do something that supports the struggling child's hope and self-confidence. The psychologist Gina Higgins says, "The surrogates of the resilient were generally available for only small amounts of clock time, and some faded after a limited developmental exposure. Yet their positive impact persisted for life."

More often than not, those surrogate helpers of resilient children—remembered over a lifetime—are found at school. The resilient generally strive to do well in school and tend to do so. Among the African Americans that Leavelle Cox studied, most reported that reading had protected them against the chaos at home. They read during family feuds, at times of internal and external upsets. The continuity of the written page was soothing.

Structuring of the mind appears to be enormously important to the resilient. It is therapeutic for the natural chaos and negativity of our ongoing thoughts, the ordinary dukkha of everyday life. All of us face the struggle to overcome background mental negativity and chaos, the state of our minds when undirected. People who are resilient from childhood trauma must have developed skill in reducing this negativity because they, more than others, have a fate that could produce overwhelming suffering. Some of this capacity comes with organizing themselves to help others and seeing their lives as having potential and meaning much larger than their own immediate needs. And some of it comes with directing attention to learning and concentration on tasks before them, on responsibilities and chores, on work to be done.

When I see people in psychotherapy who have been suffering for years from childhood adversity, I keep in mind the potential relief they'll find in being able to help others who have experienced similar miseries, and in engaging in some kind of study. Clients have often balked at my suggestion that they would benefit from disciplining their minds through further study and reading. Behind my encouragement of people to finish or continue education is the knowledge of my own and others' stories of resilience—especially the way in which study and reading brought relief from chaos and negativity and fear. People who are resilient from a difficult childhood have benefited from early self-determination, responsibility, and help offered to others.

HOPE

WHEN I ASKED Joanna Macy what gave her courage to continue talking back to her father, and later to society, she said: "I need to praise or acknowledge the little Joanna who was able to survive. She had no female models. None. Her mother acted like a doormat, but Joanna was able to defend her because Joanna didn't lose respect for herself."

She emphasized that there was something *different* about Joanna, different from the other members of her family, that made her determined to speak the truth and find a better life than that she had witnessed. "I have a great appetite for happiness, but I have had to keep choosing. I was never going to just lie down and die. I was going to try to achieve and to have a life."

This feeling different from one's family, in a way that hadn't been shown or taught, was mentioned in all four interviews I conducted for this book and in the research of Gina Higgins as well. I connect this feeling of being different with *hope*: the belief and expectation that one can have a different life from the others around one, especially when those others seem trapped in misery. Although my four friends didn't describe themselves as more hopeful than others in their families, they saw themselves as different, set apart, and thus capable of developing a different way.

Dan Gottlieb said it most strongly. He has come to see his fundamental feeling of being different as his capacity to choose life again and again over death. Dan traces his first recognition of feeling different to a moment in early childhood when he was out to dinner with family members: "We were at a restaurant. I was with my sister, my parents, and both of their mothers. My parents were arguing with their mothers about what to order—one fish has bones and one doesn't and so on. I just looked at the five of them. I said to myself, in seven-year-old language, 'These people are nuts!' I realized that I was *different* from all of them. It was lonely and frightening and sad. There was no exhilaration; in fact, I think I was a little depressed about it most of my childhood."

Dan's first recognition of difference felt nothing like hope or good luck; it was simply the sense of being set apart from the other members of his family. Later, as he traced this theme of feeling different over the years, he realized that it took on meanings from feeling "too short" in childhood to feeling alienated later as his life presented him with tragedy. Eventually, he linked up the feeling with his strong determination to live. Joining and rejoining with life has ultimately meant that Dan feels that no obstacle will totally defeat him: "It's live or die. You have to make a choice, and most people who live with trauma or suffering don't ever make that choice. They wind up in the middle." They live a life filled with dukkha—negative evaluations and discontent.

Hope

When twenty-five childhood survivors of the Holocaust—identified as resilient—were interviewed about how
they continued to engage with life, after having lost so
much, they said that they were able to do what most of us
might think is impossible: to live with unresolved mourning.
They pursued active and creative lives because they determined they would do so, in the face of constant reminders
of their losses. They saw themselves as different from others,
more able to use their concentration and focus to benefit
rather than diminish themselves and others. They explained
that as children they had learned skills for diverting their
attention from their fearful status to thoughts of hope for
the future.

Although I wouldn't reduce this feeling of difference to
one characteristic or ability, some findings show that optimism may provide a better protection against acute and
chronic stress than pessimism. By optimism, I don't mean
denial. Optimism among the resilient is an attitude that
difficulties can be overcome—and may even be worthwhile.
It is riding the mule backwards, gathering skills for working
on one's own attitude and responsibilities while developing
plans to deal with whatever stress may emerge. With optimism, one doesn't collapse into fantasies of how things are
or should be—like the man who got sick because he "saw"
a snake in his tea when it was only the reflection of a rope
hanging overhead. Instead, one keeps focused on one's own
attitude and knowledge, recognizing how suffering can be
created by the wrong attitude and that it can be alleviated
with the right one.

When the Zen master and author Philip Kapleau was

reminiscing about his childhood near the beginning of my interview with him, he said: "There was no real love. I felt different from all the rest [of my family]. I felt different from them right from the beginning." What he saw in his mother's hatred and resentment of his father, in her humiliation and cruelty toward his younger brother, was a way of life that Kapleau would disavow. Although he may have felt this only as difference at the time, later he could see that something in him was aware of other ways of being, of potential freedom from human cruelty and resentment. It took years for that something to emerge, and yet its potential began in his feeling open to a way of life different from that of his childhood.

Shibvon, the pediatric nurse in Higgins's study, was able even in her worst moments (during her fifth-grade year when her mother's lover was sexually abusing Shibvon) to disidentify with the darkness:

> I wanted to be something more than what I had, and I think that [when the sexual abuse] started up—I know it sounds bizarre—but I think in fifth grade, *I was always planning my life. I was going to get out of it. . . . It was going to get better.* [emphasis in original]

Whatever might allow the resilient to feel hopeful about developing differently, to follow a path they do not know, is not well understood but seems to be a combination of factors. It may stem from an underlying solid first year of life, without terrible impingements, combined with intelligence and a religious or spiritual context that provides a larger picture of what life is about. Some insight or intuition or knowledge allows the resilient to feel free enough to imagine a different life, one that has meaning or purpose or concern for others. Feeling different liberates the hope and the imagination in resilient children to engage more compassionately, creatively, and fully than their elders.

MEANING

Family sorrow is not only a painful wound to be endured, ana-
lyzed, and treated. It may in fact become a seed that gives birth
to our spiritual healing and awakening.

WAYNE MULLER, 1992

FINDING PURPOSE or meaning in an ordeal ties together the
themes of help and hope. Many of the resilient report that
their spirituality or religion was significant in helping them
discover a purpose in their suffering and pain, or that they
discovered a spirituality through the process of their pain.

Joanna Macy said she has never lost faith in a larger
context in life, a bigger picture than her own personal existence. "Initially my life had meaning through Christianity. I
came from a long line of preachers. My father was the first
in his family not to be a minister." At the Fifth Avenue
Presbyterian Church in New York City, Joanna first found
solace and community under the watchful eye of a minister
who always noticed and commented on her intelligence.
Participating in church "lent some orderliness and coherence
to life. The Hebrew Prophets were very, very important to
me."

One incident stands out for Joanna as she recalls how her
faith grew in childhood: "I think I was nine, and it was my

first year on my grandfather's farm, away for the whole summer. My grandfather was a preacher, but he also had a working farm. I came and sat on his lap and he quoted the Bible, from Matthew I think. 'Come unto me all ye who labor and are heavy laden, and I will give ye rest. Take my yoke upon you, for my yoke is easy and the burden is light'— something like that. I was riveted. I asked him to say it again. I couldn't believe that God, at the center of the universe, knew about the reality of pain. And my grandfather, a very saintly kind of guy, said that God knows about pain in the whole world. And I thought, Okay, I'll let him take some of mine and we'll be in this together."

Feeling that God shared with her the belief that injustice was wrong, and that He could understand why she spoke out so often against her father, helped Joanna immensely. Although she was literally alone in protests against her father, she felt supported by the universe, by God who knew about the reality of pain. Many of the resilient adults in Gina Higgins's study report the same kind of help from a spiritual context, often an informal one, that allowed them to believe in something that went beyond the miseries of their family life.

Some of the resilient from childhood adversity report mystical experiences, and others simply acknowledge a formal or informal belief that allowed them to see meaning and purpose that transcended their personal pain.

The psychologist Aaron Antonovsky—having done research on the transformation of suffering and pain—talks about the critical importance of a "sense of coherence" for renewal and resilience. This coherence is brought about by some context or relationship that allows a person in crisis or pain to

make sense of what is happening
believe that one can meet the demands of the event(s)
believe that things are generally meaningful in life

In his interviews with people who were able to continue to engage life against overwhelming odds, Antonovsky found that a strong sense of coherence helped sustain "enthusiasm." The root of *enthusiasm* is "in god," *en-theos.*

Sometimes the ordinary events of our lives awaken us to the deepest coherence. I use the following story to help people see how to appreciate the spiritual meaning in their everyday lives.

ONCE UPON A TIME an emperor decided that if he knew the answers to three questions, he would always know what to do, no matter what. The questions were these:

When is the best time to do things?
Who are the most important people?
What is the most important thing?

The emperor offered a big reward for the right answers to these questions, and he received many, but none satisfied him.

Finally, he decided to travel to the top of the mountain to visit an old hermit who would perhaps know the right answers. When he reached the hermit, the emperor asked his three questions. The hermit, digging in his garden, listened attentively and said nothing. He returned to his digging. As the emperor watched him, he noticed how tired the old man seemed.

"Here," he said, "give me the spade and I'll dig while you rest." So the hermit rested and the emperor dug.

After several hours, the emperor was very tired. He put down the spade and said: "If you can't answer my questions, that's all right. Just tell me and I'll take my leave."

"Do you hear someone running?" the hermit asked suddenly, pointing to the edge of the woods.

Sure enough, a man came tumbling out of the woods, clutching his stomach. He collapsed as the hermit and the emperor reached him. Opening the man's shirt, they saw that he had a deep cut. The emperor cleaned the wound, using his own shirt to bind it. Regaining consciousness, the man asked for water. The emperor hurried to a nearby stream and brought him some. The man drank gratefully, then slept.

The hermit and the emperor carried the man into the hut and lay him on the hermit's bed. By this time the emperor was exhausted, too, and he fell asleep.

The next morning when the emperor awoke, he saw the wounded man staring down at him.

"Forgive me," the man whispered.

"Forgive you?" said the emperor, sitting up, wide awake. "What have you done that needs my forgiveness?"

"You do not know me, your majesty, but I have thought of you as my sworn enemy. During the last war you killed my brother and took away my lands."

The man went on to explain that he had been lying in ambush, waiting for the emperor to come back down the mountain when one of the emperor's attendants recognized him as an enemy and gave him a painful wound.

"I fled, but if you hadn't helped me when you did, I surely would have died. I had planned to kill you. Instead, you saved my life! I am ashamed and very grateful."

The emperor was glad to hear the story and restored the man's land.

After the man left, the emperor looked at the hermit and said: "I must leave now. I shall travel everywhere looking for the answers to my questions."

The hermit laughed and said, "Your questions are already answered, your majesty."

The hermit explained that if the emperor had not helped to dig in the garden but had simply hurried off in search of his answers, he would have been killed on the way down the mountain.

"The most important time for you was the time you were digging in my garden. The most important person was myself, the person you were with, and the most important thing was simply to help me," added the hermit.

"And later, when we met the wounded man who came up the mountain, the most important time was that spent tending his wound, for otherwise he would have died—and you would not have become friends. And he was at that moment the most important person in the world, and the most important pursuit was tending his wound.

"The present moment is the only moment," the hermit continued. "The most important person is always the person you are with. And the most important pursuit is making the person standing at your side happy. What could be simpler or more important?"

TO ATTAIN THE REAL and immediate ability to pay attention to the present moment and be truly effective in offering help, most of us have to be sustained by some belief system that takes us beyond ourselves.

Joanna Macy feels she has always had a spiritual context, beginning with her roots in Christianity and leading eventually to her deep involvement with Buddhism. When I asked her what meaning she sees in suffering, she answered: "I see suffering as a bridge to interaction with the world and other people. It is where you find the strongest sense of mutual belonging. We all have suffering in common. If you think your suffering is private, you need to open up and experience what your brothers and sisters are suffering. We can define a broader vision of who we are through our pain."

The apparent spiritual renewal in North America that is currently much broadcast by the news media may be a response to the despair of our society. Pollution, overcrowding, homelessness, crime in our cities, and our inability (or unwillingness) to control the use of weapons in our streets may unconsciously convey to us all a feeling of impending disaster. To retain a sense of coherence about our lives, we need some kind of spiritual fabric that holds us together when life is too painful.

Carl Jung believed that some kind of enduring spiritual belief was necessary for psychological health. As I said earlier, Jung noted the process of transformation that seems to underlie a lifetime's development: the most difficult becomes the most developmental; that which is presented as pain and misery is often the challenge that gives us purpose. Jung felt confident also, before having any access to empirical findings about resilience, that childhood adversity often opens the way of adult development. Rather than seeing adversity as simply bad or merely the cause of later neurosis, he believed that the *conscious attitude* (especially the attitude of the adult looking back) is the key to "individuation" or personal development. Different from Freud, who believed that psychotherapy works directly to recover or uncover the forgotten history of the individual, Jung believed that psychotherapy transforms the current conscious attitude so that the past can be seen differently, so that the life can be retold within a broader context.

From Jung's point of view, for the individual to develop through misery and suffering—in psychotherapy or not—a spiritual context must be present, one that allows hope and coherence to be sustained during the time of acute pain, and then later when suffering is likely to recur. The emperor in the story seeks out the hermit as someone who is supposed to know the answers to critical questions, the secrets of wisdom and transcendence. Without this kind of resource—a view that lends a larger perspective to the momentary event—Jung felt it was impossible to make the full development from suffering to creative purpose. Spirituality and religion provide the methods and means of *translating* meaning from an individual level to a universal or transcendent one.

Meaning

Joanna Macy puts the idea this way: "From my own experience in Buddhism, and its teaching of interdependence and mutual belonging, I would say that we are One, like jewels in the Net of Indra—a mythic image of netted jewels where each one reflects the others and the whole so you can look at any one and see everything. When you open your capacity to experience pain, and bow to it, you can see all of life itself. Then you can let go of constricting self-definitions and old ways of interpreting reality. There is no birth of consciousness without pain and no growth of consciousness without pain."

Spiritual or religious beliefs are often cited by the resilient as vehicles for transcending hate, bitterness, and envy. Not everyone has a direct spiritual experience in becoming resilient, but most people describe a major transformative event associated with their pain or abuse. Some kind of grounding belief assures order and dignity under the strain of chaos and disintegration.

HIDDEN BENEFITS

THROUGHOUT THIS PART of the book, I have been pointing out the possible motivational and spiritual resources in childhood adversity. Although none of us would ask for a difficult childhood, when we've had one then we have much to gain from seeing how it might bring with it the strengths and potentials that the resilient clearly show.

Before leaving this topic, I want to address one childhood factor that has turned up some surprising results in studies of resilience: gender difference.

We know from a number of studies that throughout childhood and adolescence, girls tend to underestimate their achievements and believe that their successes are due to hard work and luck instead of ability. Boys, however, tend to overestimate their performances in everything from athletics to scholastics—and believe that their success is due to ability and intelligence. Although these are generalizations from large studies, they say something about the overall picture of advantages and disadvantages based on gender.

From these and other studies, we also know that boys and girls receive different treatment in the classroom, from elementary school through college. Boys receive more criticism and praise, are asked more challenging questions, and are given more instruction, on the whole, than girls. In this way they are taught to sharpen their ideas and find their voices, and even to achieve more. Girls learn that they should be quiet and polite, defer to authorities—and to boys' views— and that they should relinquish their ambitions in favor of using the "power" of their appearances. Much has been written about girls' losses of self-confidence and achievement and voice as they enter adolescence from childhood, and about their difficulties in building them back again in adulthood.

These losses appear to carry over into adulthood, since women are significantly more likely than men to say they need help with depression and they generally score higher on measures of distress such as depression or hopelessness. They are more likely than men to have sexual abuse in their backgrounds. These hidden truths may lead to alienation that is reinforced by social situations in which their contributions and challenges may be trivialized or disregarded.

The psychologist and Jungian analyst June Singer felt this kind of alienation during fifteen years of her first marriage. Since her adolescence she had been experiencing periodic weakness and fatigue. The cause was undiagnosed, and the symptoms were dismissed as neurotic excuses for avoiding activities she didn't enjoy. Married to a man of great energy, vitality, and verbal facility, she became quiet and retiring. "I felt I couldn't compete with him. I rarely spoke up in a group. I felt that I could not function with integrity in expressing my real self. As I look back on that time, I realize that I must have been depressed, maybe even clinically depressed."

Although the female gender seems clearly to carry distinct disadvantages in regard to our cultural images of achievement and self-confidence, in studies of childhood adversity girls are generally more resilient than boys (in the absence of harm to the primary caregiver). As in many other areas, our fundamental sense of "disadvantage" is shifted through the study of resilience. In regard to this special area of development—dealing with childhood adversity—girls have the advantage.

Boys show more symptoms of aggression under stress; they are more disruptive and impulsive. Girls show more anxiety and depression, internalizing rather than externalizing the stresses of chaotic environments. The lessons of resilience from childhood adversity seem to hint that growing up female has hidden benefits. Ironically, the constraints placed on female children seem to result in problems that are more internal than external, more likely to bring them to a therapist's office than a prison, and more likely to keep them out of the punitive cycle of street life. The advantages provided to male children can make them vulnerable to unreachable expectations and set them off course for coping with the ordinary limitations and losses of life.

We don't yet know enough about what enhances resilience to be sure about what is helpful and what is not helpful in gender practices. We don't know whether masculine socialization for competition and control fares better in the face of adversity, or whether feminine socialization for restraint and self-effacement does.

We certainly know that human development is strongly buffered by stable caregivers. Warm family interactions, responsible child care, and internal resources (such as intelligence and easy temperament) play important roles in providing the strengths and securities that carry over in the face of adversity. We also know that low self-esteem, lack of self-determination, and hopelessness bode poorly for resilience.

Overt and covert messages to girls and women that they are no better than their appearance, that they are no stronger than their popularity, and that their intelligence and assertions don't count—all these must undermine resilience, unravel the binding together of strengths and resources that every resilient person needs in the face of loss and pain.

To be positively engaged with challenge and to receive the feedback that your efforts are working is perhaps one major ingredient of resilience. As both the resilient and those who study them say, the ability to find meaning and purpose in the face of adversity is what prepares us for further development. The groundwork for this condition has some mix of help, hope, and meaning, although not in the way that many people imagine.

The ideal childhood for a resilient, purposeful adult life may not be the happiest, the most secure, the most privileged. It may not include two ideal parents, the best educational opportunities, the best possible preparation for a highly competitive world. But it must include some kindness, even if only a passing kindness. It must include enough food, housing, and clothing to keep together mind and body. It must include some witnessing of love, whether love given or love received. It must include plenty of opportunity for self-determination, some fundamental self-respect, and enough return for one's efforts in helping others to be able to give more. There must be opportunities to use the abundance of one's gifts—whether those are talents or talking back or creativity or practical skills.

What seems to count most for resilience is the opportunity to encounter pain within a context of meaning and to find that one's compassion (one's suffering-with) has power. These sustain an underlying belief that the world is good and in order.

From those who are resilient from childhood adversity, we learn that help is often valuable to the giver as much as to the receiver. We learn that giving help in childhood, even to a parent who is ambivalently loved, can be the first step toward a purpose in life. We also learn that a ubiquitous sense of being different, feeling like an outsider or deviant, in a family that is hostile or abusive or even uncompassionate, may be the seed of hope. The belief that a better life is possible arises during misery and pain when we can feel ourselves to be "other" or beyond the immediate context as though we are protected by a magic circle drawn in the sand. To become resilient and to use pain for transformation, we must expand and support this hope with a larger context of meaning, usually a spiritual context, that permits us to translate deficits and losses into potentials for new development.

PART FOUR

Letting the Self Die

The question is not who is better or more honest, but who will gain more freedom from all fear, who will gain the peace and joy that the masters have spoken of.

GEORGE FOWLER, 1995

WHEN PEOPLE SUFFER from dissatisfaction and a lack of purpose, they often search for something unique and enduring in their identity—a True Self. Maybe they've heard or read the lingo that some people have problems with a "false self," and they look forward to being able to say "This is the real me" or something similar. There are many cultural assumptions about the uniqueness of individuality in our society, and many adults look to psychotherapy for a true or authentic self.

Ironically, I understand the goal of this kind of search to be almost the opposite of discovering a True Self. To identify and take responsibility for your suffering and transform it into a purpose, you will surely need to let the self—and the whole idea of *an* authentic self—die. In its place will be an honoring of *change* as the basis of life, and impermanence as the basis of self.

LETTING THE SELF DIE

The basic human tendency to make "things" out of passing moods or processes, especially to make a "self" out of changing subjective states and roles, is considered "ignorance" in Buddhism. It is ignorance of the ceaselessly changing, interdependent reality of life.

A particularly painful aspect of our ignorance is the belief that we have or can find a True Self that will be permanent and everlasting. To ignore impermanence, to hang onto things as they are at this moment or to try to make them what we want, is to create more suffering. One reason that many of us have anguish over death is that we fail to keep in mind the truth of the impermanence of ourselves and others, all around us. As a Tibetan Buddhist teacher says, "The realization of impermanence is paradoxically the only thing we can hold onto, perhaps our only lasting possession." For us in the West, especially, it is often hard to embrace the impermanence of the self and to grasp the idea that the self is a function, not a thing.

To make the translation from the idea of a self as something existing somewhere to the idea of a self as function (interdependent even, on other people), we first have to give up the notion of a True Self. When I talk about this with my colleagues in psychoanalysis—some of whom speak passionately of a True Self philosophy—I'm often asked if this whole business about "self" isn't just a matter of language. Aren't we all talking about the same goal, to engage life spontaneously and authentically, whether or not we use the language of True Self?

I don't think so. When people believe strongly in a True Self, they tend to hang onto powerful emotional moments as though they were more real, more substantial, than other moments of self. They want to say, "*Now* I've got it. Now I know who I am, and I need only to go back to this and everything else will fall into place." This is very different from understanding yourself as *always* in process, whether in big moments or small, and always depending on many conditions and other beings in order to exist. On the pop psychology scene, some people who follow the True Self philosophy fall into identifying themselves with one or two psychological complexes—like the victim child or the hero complex—because the associated strong emotions seem to express truth. To direct your attention to what is before you and to the people around you without evaluating what is "most important," as the hermit in the story says, is the only way to break free of fears that increase pain and suffering.

Instead of talking about a search for a True Self or any kind of self, I find it most useful to see the self as a function sustained by connection and compassion. To attain wholeness of being, to reside in love rather than fear, we must be able to use pain and suffering to discover a purpose in being here. Under these conditions, the central integrating function of self can reach to its widest possible parameters. It can include all life. When this experience of interdependence is deeply known, it is connected with some spiritual practice. Ordinary adversity can be the first step on a path that opens the door to a new way of seeing ourselves, of becoming stable and secure in a new order that is more enduring and connected than an isolated self.

To live with the impermanence of the self is no small task. Most of us resist change, even if our resistance leads to disaster or a kind of half-life of envy and self-pity. And yet there are times when we must die to an old identity if we want to survive wholly. If there is adversity in childhood, we may have to give up a certain dependence or lighthearted-ness and develop discrimination and helpfulness early. If there is a catastrophe in adulthood—a sudden loss or in-jury—we have to give up our old expectations or we'll be doomed to be "survivors" who never thrive. Most such turn-ing points are not welcome. The necessity to change usually feels like an intrusion.

Jungian analyst June Singer describes the role of distress in the process of human development this way: "I believe that suffering is a major change agent. It certainly has been that for me. Other factors may make for change, but there's no doubt in my mind that when a situation feels truly unbearable, some part of our being has to give way.

"When things get intolerable we can no longer maintain the facade that holds us together. At first we experience ourselves as disorganized, chaotic. We have to reorganize in some way in order to survive. We can move forward by recognizing that the past is behind us, and try to find a new sense of self. Or we can stay stuck in ruminating over past events and try to recapture a self that is no longer as useful as it was. You can either fundamentally transform yourself or you can get mired down in what Jung called a 'negative restoration of the persona,' an attempt to revive the old appearances. You just cover up and pretend that nothing's happened. Embracing the new self requires that we engage directly with our lives as they are in the very moment that pain or suffering seems intolerable. Trying to keep up old appearances, on the other hand, invites a feeling of deadness, of depression."

When June was a young wife and mother in her twenties and thirties, she could not acknowledge to anyone the pain she was experiencing—both physical and emotional pain. This quiet suffering became a wall between herself and others. Today she knows very well how important it is to face pain and to accept it as one of life's realities that cannot be denied without causing serious consequences.

When I interviewed her in her office in Palo Alto, California, June was reluctant to talk about some of this. She had not spoken publicly about her twenty-one-year marriage to the rabbi and psychologist Richard Singer. When he died thirty-five years ago, June was filled with unresolved anger and frustration, but over the years she had come to understand that the man she had blamed for their unhappiness had been suffering as much as she. "In his position as a clergyman and confidante, he had access to the spiritual and sexual longings of many women, and from time to time he would enter into clandestine relationships with one or another of them. He must have found it difficult to resist these women, for whom he embodied so much that they probably found missing in their own personal lives and marriages. I suspected. I felt at times that I knew. When I hinted at what I suspected, he always denied it. But I did not understand the degree of conflict he was experiencing. His personality was such and mine was such that he would make all kinds of protestations and I would start to feel that maybe I was crazy, that I wasn't seeing what I was seeing."

Why did she remain in the marriage? "I was afraid of being

left, of being deserted with no resources. I felt quite isolated and my teenage daughter had her own problems. I wasn't sure I could manage."

June didn't yet have the talking-back voice that Joanna Macy developed from childhood on. Like so many women in her generation—June is in her seventies now—she felt silenced.

WE ARE CHALLENGED countless times to let an old self die during what we regard as a life span. At first we do it almost naturally, as biological processes demand the reorganization of our personalities and perceptions. From the earliest infantile prostrate self emerges the active self of the toddler. The impulsive toddler then gives way to a more cautious child. The conforming child eventually is transformed into a self-conscious, nonconforming adolescent. At each juncture from infancy to childhood to adolescence, an old self is surrendered and a new self is born. Sometimes we feel acutely the sacrifice of the old, as when we mourn the loss of magical thinking when it is exchanged for valuable rational and practical (but far less romantic) methods of understanding the world. At other times we are happy to let the old slip away, as when we see the physical signs of puberty and realize that we are catching up to our peers in looking "grown up."

At first, change seems natural in life. But later, as biological growth slows down, the requirements to change appear to diminish, and most of us habituate to certain expectations about ourselves and the world. There are no longer physical transitions as obvious signals.

Instead the changes become more a matter of choice—psychological and social transitions such as leaving home for a new partnership, developing a work life, perhaps having our own children. Eventually we encounter death and loss as our parents die and our children move away. These subtler changes and all of their in-between transitions may seem easy to ignore or oppose. Some people hold onto youthful appearances through various kinds of manipulations of their bodies and faces. Some people retain the less structured life of adolescence rather than surrender to the structured schedule demanded with adult responsibilities. Some people acquire a lot of material resources, and ever more youthful partners, hoping to stave off fears of illness or death. Some people cling to childhood expectations of finding perfect relationships. But all along the way, unexpected miseries and accidents can confront us suddenly with the necessity to change.

Radio talk show host Dan Gottlieb recalls that he held onto depression, rage, and shame for almost two years after his accident. He couldn't give up his old self—the able-bodied Dan.

During his initial stay at the hospital where surgery was performed to prevent further injury to his spinal cord after his neck was broken, Dan had some preliminary physical therapy to restore the use of some of his shoulder and arm muscles in movements of his arms side to side and up and down. Six weeks of lying inert in various kinds of casts and devices had dissipated Dan's few functional muscles. So he had to practice turning the pages of a book while his arms hung marionettelike from devices that held them up from the ceiling. "Because I worked so hard, by the end of the week I was able to turn pages without these antigravity devices. My muscles had built up so much. The physical therapist put her arms around me and said, 'Are you proud of yourself that you can do this?' and I cried. I said, 'A few years ago I wrote a 350-page doctoral dissertation. You want me to be proud that I can turn a page in a book?'

"Two years later, after the physical therapy incident, I was in my office and I was reading an article Xeroxed from a journal, stapled in the upper left corner. I was trying to move it from my filing cabinet to my desk and it began to fall. I eased it down to the floor, holding it to the side of the cabinet so that the staple was up in the air like a tepee. Then I maneuvered until I got my thumb up underneath and was able to lift it back up to my desk. This whole process took about twenty minutes. I felt enormous pride, and then I thought, What's the difference between this and turning pages? The difference is that now I'm quadriplegic, and *then* I was still—in my view of myself—an able-bodied man who couldn't even turn a page in a book."

It takes more than pain or trauma to bring about the death of an old self; it takes a change of attitude. When Dan held onto the old able-bodied self, he was filled with negative emotions, especially shame. Often he was angry that he had even lived. But when he took on the full meaning of his quadriplegic self, Dan discovered a clarity of mind and purpose he hadn't previously known. His compassionate nature, often hidden by narcissism and compensations in the old Dan, was now able to shine.

In a large study of people who were resilient after great difficulties, we find traces of this transformation of self. Adversity truly faced becomes incorporated into the self, a new identity. For civil rights workers, dangerous and debilitating experiences later became valued lifelong aspects of their identities, told and retold as parts of who they were. Long-lived cancer patients, who had successfully survived childhood cancers, accepted their cancers as part of themselves, as part of life and health, not as something separate and threatening. People who grew up competently after a childhood with a mentally ill parent saw their parents' illnesses as a part of who they (the children) had become. What they had witnessed early gave them lifetime insights into themselves and others. In all three of these groups a major shift in the self, incorporating the illness or pain into one's identity, helped people to continue to engage fully in their lives without resentment.

In describing his initial confrontation with his own Parkinson's disease, Zen master—Roshi (meaning venerable teacher)—Kapleau says that he suddenly became aware that he and the illness were one. They would be living together for the remainder of his life. "An insight came to me: the disease is now yours, it's inseparable from you. The only way, it seemed to me, to deal with a chronic disease is to accept it as part of you, as part of your life, not something isolated that you just have a marginal relationship with." This recognition opened his curiosity and interest in finding out about the disease.

YET MOST PEOPLE fail to embrace their adversities, to engage fully with life after pain and suffering. As Dan Gottlieb said, they tend to live a kind of half-life, hanging onto an old self that no longer works, not fully engaging in the new one.

There are many ways to resist change throughout adult life, and I've seen most of them in psychotherapy. Apart from the pathological effects of trauma and abuse, most resistance has to do with fantasies about how the world and others should treat us. It is rooted in ideals—for perfection, beauty, love, security—that turn into dukkha, suffering and negativity, when they are held too tightly or are too exaggerated and grandiose. Great expectations, even our most humane visions for the future, can throw us off balance and become a barrier to development when we regard them as more important than what stands before us.

When we insist on our fantasies, we are flooded by agitations, feelings of resentment and self-pity. We see ourselves through the lenses of our childhood complexes and get stuck feeling like the archetypal victim or retaliating like the archetypal terrible parent. This is neurosis, the useless suffering that interferes with the necessity to change.

A woman in her middle forties whose mother had died soon after her own birth came to me in therapy with angry demands about wanting a better life than she had. She was already somewhat aware that she repeatedly created conditions in which those who truly loved her were not able to express it directly. She unintentionally "forced" people to abandon her again and again by holding them at arm's length and speaking to them only of her criticisms, blame, and demands.

Two and a half years later, this woman had learned to stop treating others aggressively. She had begun to see how she had created some of the problems that had bothered her. Now she spoke openly about her needs and concerns without blaming others. She had begun to change, but she had not changed her old self. She was soon to encounter it full force.

She and I had reached a point where she felt her dependence on *me.* This aroused fear that I might not be able to help her successfully finish therapy so that she could become independent of me. Instead of telling me about this fear (for which she really had no words), she simply attacked our therapy for not helping her—for "not really changing anything." When I would try to shed some light on how therapy had helped or how she was now holding *me* at arm's length with criticism, she simply felt blamed.

Empathically, I could see how hard it would be for this woman to let her old self die. Her old self was wrapped in a victim complex: no one else she knew personally had had to endure the kind of pain she'd had, and so no one could really know her pain because she had lost her mother at birth. Now she suspected that I might be like all the others, unable to understand her deeply, because I had not lost my mother at birth.

She had often felt alienated and enraged throughout her life, and she had rationalized a great many of her attacks on others based on this victim stance. If she were to give up this self, how could she ever justify the actions that had wrecked those other relationships? Yet to hold onto the old victim self would also mean great pain because she would have to face still another failure (with me), this time with someone she had felt to be a "trustworthy expert." Hers was the deep dilemma that often precedes a shedding of an old self.

After months of hanging onto her old self, my client tearfully recognized how fundamentally she had created and re-created so much pain and difficulty throughout her life. She saw now how she had directed a drama (in which she also starred) of abandonment and loss, in which she had unconsciously invited others to play the parts of abandoning mother or unempathic father.

After she dissolved her identification with the old victim self, she discovered that she could help others with her newfound understanding. When others around her became envious or blaming, she had a new patience in listening to them without taking their blame literally. She used her new skills at work, and then at home, and she began to feel loved and appreciated by people around her. Seeing how her dependence on me was part of the drama that she had created, and how it had become a test of whether or not I truly understood her, she was able to leave therapy contentedly.

By the time she left, she recognized how long she had held onto the idea that the most essential thing about her was the fact that she didn't have a mother. Suppressing a knowledge of her strengths, she had kept many people at arm's length, testing whether they could understand her pain. As she developed a new self, one that was grounded in feeling lovable and more loving, she could fully appreciate the love she received.

No Essential Self

ONE REASON WHY it is so hard for old selves to die is that we in Western society hold strong beliefs that we are solid, separate selves, basic entities housed in our own little bodies. We see ourselves as being essentially like this or that. Many of us even label ourselves by psychological categories: "I'm a depressive type" or "I'm a feeling type" or "I'm a child of an alcoholic." In this way we make permanent states of passing emotions or complexes. People say "This is who I am, I've always been this way and I'll never change," and they feel proud of the claim.

Growing up in Western society, we have learned languages and cultural practices that enforce the value and ideal of an individual, permanent self. *I, me, mine, you, yours, us,* and *them* are pronouns richly scattered through our sentences. We speak (and relate our life stories) as though we were entirely independent of others, and it is hard for us to see how the self is a function and not a thing. Not all cultures or all people define the self as being so individual, as depending exclusively on one brain and one body.

In her 1991 book about Buddhism and social action, Joanna Macy says:

> The way we define . . . the self is arbitrary. We can place it between our ears and have it looking out from our eyes, or we can widen it to include the air we breathe, or at other moments, we can cast its boundaries farther to include the oxygen-giving trees and plankton, our external lungs, and beyond them the web of life in which they are sustained.

When we experience the self as a function, then we begin to feel our interdependence on everything else and to see how we merge into all that surrounds us. This is close to what Buddhism teaches about "no-self" and what Jung meant when he regarded the self as an empty center. To begin to appreciate the no-self, we have to surrender many of our ordinary beliefs about the uniqueness and boundaries of a self.

This process begins with seeing how we convince ourselves that we have an essential self. All people have a strong tendency to develop this belief, although some societies and cultures promote a softening and dissolving of it. Belief in an essential self begins with self-consciousness, the sense of being a separate self in control of itself, that takes root in the second year of life.

Although each of us is a center of organized action and perception as an infant, in infancy we're not clear about the boundaries of our bodies or the influence of our emotions and desires. Things just happen to us. Emotions come and go, images come and go, and we're not anywhere in particular, not entirely embodied in our skin.

The psychological experience of being a separate self—a discrete entity of thought and action—emerges gradually out of infancy. It becomes full-blown somewhere between eighteen months and two years. Toddlers tell us about it: "Mine!" and "No!" and "Me do it!" They feel the powerful onset of individual will and the experience of directing actions.

Around this time comes the birth of self-conscious emotions—pride, shame, guilt, embarrassment, jealousy, envy. The earlier emotions, present from birth, are often called the "primary emotions," and the self-conscious ones have been dubbed "secondary." Although many animals share with us the experience of discrete primary emotions (such as joy, sadness, curiosity, disgust, fear, and aggression), whether animals feel self-conscious in the same way we humans do is debatable. Often what we admire in animals is their clear connection to primary emotion without self-consciousness. When self-conscious emotions are aroused, they stir egotism and self-protection: I matter more than you do. Most of the time when adults feel defensive and self-protective, they are engaged in self-conscious emotions. They are ashamed or guilty or proud.

It appears that human beings are wired up to create a separate self. From studies of human beings in many cultures, the psychologist Rom Harré concludes that all peoples describe some experience of "individual subjectivity" in their sense of being a person. This means that people everywhere feel themselves to be the authors of their own actions, feel embodied in their own bodies—seeing themselves as continuous over time—and feel themselves as the seat of emotion. These conditions of personal will, coherence, and continuity comprise what I would call the "function" of self or individual subjectivity.

Having a self means being able to experience oneself as the subject of one's own desires and actions. We develop the function of self through our relationships with other selves, with other people. We fill out the meaning of self through the influences of what other people, at first our families and later our communities, tell us. But most of us assume that the self is a thing rather than a function and that it exists somewhere—in the space between our eyes, perhaps, or elsewhere in our bodies.

This tendency, like the one to label ourselves with a technical psychological term, is a way that we define ourselves. We pick out certain moods or abilities and turn them into identities, almost substances. I'm a passive person. I'm a rational type. This is not the same as referring to ourselves in terms of the roles we fill, such as I'm a mother or father. Rather, it is a grasping onto a particular passing quality and making it into the essence of who we are. (We can do this with our roles, too, but often it is clear that no role completely encompasses who we are.) We do not allow ourselves to be fully who we are; we want a definition of a self that exists and continues.

To a large extent, this tendency is adaptive in our society because we see it as taking responsibility for ourselves. We want to name who we are and to distinguish the self so that we can claim personal responsibility for our moods or values or actions—which would be fine, if it didn't carry over into believing that this is only and exactly who we are. Many people unknowingly or knowingly believe that they should defend themselves by labeling their values, preferences, and weaknesses as unchanging personal characteristics. They constrain themselves to fit a certain identity. Then they won't ever have to be "someone else," to change their habits or ideas, to develop into a new self.

Sometimes Westerners associate the notion of an impermanent self, as it is discussed in Buddhism especially, with some kind of negative commentary on ego functions—those skills and abilities we all need to navigate ourselves in the world. Often this is because some Buddhist texts translate the idea of a "separate self" as the term "ego." Thus certain prejudices have developed among Westerners who believe that Buddhism eschews or denigrates ego functions. This is a misinterpretation. It is the idea of a separate unchanging self, of holding oneself apart from others, that is the problem Buddhism brings to our attention.

The degree of privacy, separateness, and individuality regarded as healthy for the self does vary a great deal from culture to culture. In some societies, the self is experienced more strongly as part of a group or a family. There are various accounts of tribal and honor-based societies in which less emphasis is placed on personal claims of uniqueness and individuality than in our society. In one such language (according to Harré) there are no personal pronouns at all—only verb forms that indicate "the action comes from here" or "the action comes from there." But even in societies in which identity is more collective or shared (such as in some

Buddhist cultures), people *still* experience themselves as embodied, as existing over time in separate bodies and as being the authors of their actions. All people have a tendency to create an image of an essential self and to defend and protect that image, even at their own peril.

In Jung's terminology, we can call the self an archetype: universally all human beings develop and hold onto an experience of separate identity around which a single, coherent image of "me" develops. This ensures that human beings will develop as embodied, continuous, intentional, and emotional beings, and it is true of people everywhere. But the degree to which the individual self is regarded as boundaried or shared, private or public, unique or collective, changing or unchanging, is a matter of society and culture—and is an important difference between people.

Western societies have a strong tendency to see the self as stable, separate, independent, and private. Emphasizing the self as essential and unique, rather than as changing and shared, ours is a society of individualism. Our cultural focus is on individual rights and private lives. Seeing ourselves as "captains" of our little body-ships, we believe that we should make decisions and choices with our own private welfare in first place—a sort of self-promoting philosophy, as though taking care of someone else would take something away from the self.

This illusion of full control over a known self tends to obscure the fact that we are all motivated by many different impulses and ideas, conscious and unconscious. No one could experience directly the complexity of all our conflicting motivations; without unconscious filters we would be overwhelmed. I read of an experiment once—the source of which I cannot recall—that illustrates the ordinary fiction of a "unitary self" that we carry around.

A group of people were put under a mild hypnotic trance by an experimenter who gave them the posthypnotic suggestion to crawl around on the floor when the trance ended. When he called them out of the trance, the whole group began one by one to crawl around on the floor. When they were questioned by the researcher about why they were crawling, everyone had an explanation: "I've dropped something and I'm looking for it" or "I thought I saw an interesting spot there on the floor" and so on. They couldn't recall the posthypnotic suggestion because it was suppressed, but each person made up a reason for her or his actions, so as not to be stuck without an explanation. How many times a day do we find ourselves in the same situation—launching actions or speeches that may be motivated by something of which we are unconscious?

Experiencing the self as a function, not as a discrete, knowable, permanent *thing*, is part of the no-self that Buddhism teaches. I recently discovered a useful metaphor for it: the human pancreas. The pancreas changes all of its cells every twenty-four hours; every day we have a new pancreas. Yet every day the pancreas carries out roughly the same functions, although it is affected by what goes through it, by what it absorbs. Like the pancreas, the self is reconstituted every day as a new self, and yet its functions are the same: to help us integrate complexity into unity, to feel that we exist over time, and to provide us with the basic ego functions of willing, choosing, taking initiative.

When I accompany people through a course of psychotherapy in which they awaken to the roots of suffering and pain, they often reach the conclusion that the "center" or self is empty. Jung also reached this conclusion near the end of his life, when he described the final goal of our development as the discovery or intuition of an "empty center." Although we cannot directly grasp the empty center through our ordinary ego functions (that keep us organized in daily life), we can intuit or infer it through the repeated necessity to die to an old self throughout the life span. The process of deep transformation required to live fully leads us to question or dismiss the notion of an essential self, if we remain open to what is asked of us.

As Jung says at the end of his autobiography,

> there is so much that fills me: plants, animals, clouds, day and night, and the eternal in man. The more uncertain I have felt about myself, the more there has grown up in me a feeling of kinship with all things.

Eventually we are persuaded by our experiences that there is no essential way to be, no *thing* that resides at the core of our being; there is only the ongoing function of engaging with others around us and the tasks at hand.

LETTING HER OLD SELF DIE

JUNE SINGER WAS BORN in Cleveland, Ohio, in 1918 to a mother who had not finished high school, but who devoured every bit of literature she could get her hands on. "My mother was a freelance writer for magazines and for the *Cleveland Plain Dealer*, the local daily paper. She was one of the first woman journalists in her city. By the time I was twelve, her assignments often took her out of town to interview public figures from movie stars to murderesses. I admired her energy, envied her adventures. She was clever, charming, and ambitious. She was my first teacher, inspiring me with a love for good books. But it was at her hands that I had the first crucial experience with suffering that I can remember.

"My school held a contest for the best essay on 'thrift.' I conceived the idea of writing a long narrative poem called Thrift Throughout the Ages.' I labored hard over this work, and when it was finished I showed it to my mother. She made several suggestions and rewrote a few lines for me. My poem won first prize, and I was *devastated*. I felt terrible that I was getting credit for doing something that I had not done altogether on my own. The newspaper photographer asked me to come down and have my picture taken because they wanted to do a story on me, and though I wanted to refuse, my mother insisted that I go. My guilt ate at my heart! I promised myself then and there that I would show my mother that I could write without her help. And so out of that suffering came my determination to be a writer. For many years I refused to show my writing to anyone while it was still in process."

June's father was an alternative role model. "He was steady and loyal, a good provider, but not ambitious in the way that Mother was. He was a dentist, and his patients were often very poor people; some of them paid their bills by painting our house or fixing our car. But he was dominated by Mother, who thought of herself as an intellectual and saw herself as superior to him. When she'd speak to him in ways that would humiliate him, I would think to myself that when I got married I'd never do that to my husband."

In some ways the man June married at age twenty-one was much like her mother. Charming, flamboyant, intelligent, and articulate, he dominated her as her mother had dominated her father. Yet there was a difference. "I had enough of Mother in me to realize that I had within me the possibility of being a creative person, but at the same time I knew that Richard preferred to keep me in the background. He had just completed his rabbinical training when we married. Though I loved him very much, I did not like being forced into the circumscribed life of a rabbi's wife. It was like wearing shoes that were too small, only it was not my feet but my spirit that was cramped. I felt that he was jealous of any talents I had, and that he chafed when I criticized him for any reason.

"After our daughter was born, I was isolated at home with her while he was busily pursuing his congregational and other activities. Rumors reached me that he was more than attentive to other women, but when I raised the subject, he would not only deny any such thing but suggest that I was imagining things. I almost began to believe that I really was paranoid. So there was this painful uncertainty that grew in me. The worst of it was that I was not sure whether the evidence of my senses was right or not. I began to feel unreal. I knew that I must find a way to get out of the situation. But, like so many women of that time, I was economically dependent on my husband and not strong enough internally to change that."

Help came when a physician diagnosed June's physical difficulties (low energy and general malaise) as a chronic kidney infection. The offending kidney was surgically removed. After that she was free of physical pain and her energy returned.

Shortly thereafter, Richard decided to return to graduate school to work toward a Ph.D. in psychology. He may have thought that this would provide him with a graceful way to change professions. When June expressed a wish to go to graduate school herself (for a master's in psychology), he agreed. They had a tacit understanding by then that their marriage might not last, and it made sense that she should develop a profession that would enable her to support herself. She was beginning to move toward the reorganization of her personality that might transform her suffering into work that could be helpful to others.

June began to encounter the meaning of her suffering when she entered Jungian analysis in Zurich, Switzerland, in 1960. By that time Richard had left his career as a rabbi and had entered a training program to become a Jungian analyst at the C. G. Jung Institute in Zurich. June had accompanied him, along with their daughter, who was sixteen. June saw her analysis as her last chance to repair a failing relationship.

June recalled the initial dream she had as she began her personal analysis. "I was lying on a butcher's block with my hands and feet tied down. Somebody was standing over me with a big knife pointed down at my guts. I realized that I was about to be cut open, and although I was horrified, I was submitting to it." The dream suggests the agony that can accompany our determination to face the truth about ourselves or our condition. It is nothing less than "a little death." It is reminiscent of Abraham standing over his son Isaac, ready to sacrifice him as an act of faith. June says, "There is no way to falter when you have heard a call and committed yourself to a process."

In the course of her analysis, she realized that her husband's deceits and his calculating use of power amounted to what would today be called "emotional abuse." His demands on their daughter for perfectionist behavior had resulted in her becoming tense and anxious. Gradually June began to fight back. On one memorable occasion, she wanted to attend a lecture at the Jung Institute and Richard insisted that she stay home and prepare a meal for his friends. She refused and left for the lecture in angry protest. When she returned, Richard said nothing about it. The lion's claws had, it seemed, been dulled considerably, and June's old tentative self was on the block.

Throughout June's therapy in Zurich, she had been gaining strength to leave Richard. She knew that even during his analysis and training there, he was furtively seeing other women. Their daughter, understandably upset by the stress of leaving home and trying to adapt to a strange country and a foreign language, was getting little support from her parents; she underwent a brief but acute psychotic episode. When this happened to her daughter, June felt that her whole past life was crumbling, but, at the same time, the foundation for a new one was being constructed. To build a strong structure on an insubstantial base is impossible. Suffering provides the motivation for making a radical change that is needed, but that motivation in itself is not enough for new growth to take place. There also must be the right situation and the courage to seize the opportunity.

When June and Richard returned to the States, she felt emotionally ready, but still too financially dependent, to leave. Richard had resumed his questionable relationships and his denial of them to June. She was now openly furious with him, and although she confronted him with her plans to leave, she did not move out. Their daughter, now twenty-one, was living away from home, unwilling to return to the tense atmosphere that had contributed earlier to her emotional disturbance. Although both June and Richard were now Jungian psychoanalysts, they had to take positions as therapists in public agencies in order to earn a salary until they could establish a private practice. They had sold their home and spent all of their money on their training in Zurich, so that they went into debt to furnish the Chicago apartment they occupied on their return.

And then the totally unpredictable happened. As June tells it, "One day Richard came home early from work and telephoned me to say his car had gotten stuck in the snow and he'd been shoveling himself out when he felt ill. When I came home I found him very pale and complaining of sudden pain in his chest. I helped him to bed, called for emergency service, but before they came he was dead. His last words were 'Take off my shoes.' I wondered to myself, Is this the rabbi coming to stand on holy ground at last?"

June's immediate reaction was one of relief. Fate had intervened to dissolve the marriage quickly and irrevocably. She felt afraid, though, because now she would have to assume responsibility for the debts they had incurred, and she wondered how she would make a life on her own. And there was also grief—for this partner of a lifetime and for the hopes for change in a relationship that now could never be realized.

But change did occur in surprising ways. The few people who had been seeing Richard for analysis now came to June to express their sorrow and loss; over and over she helped them work through their separation from the therapist in whom they had placed trust and confidence. By being fully present with them in their grief and feelings of abandonment, June began to see her own pain as a tool for helping others. Almost without exception, Richard's former clients in therapy now elected to become clients of June. They were immediately connected to her by a strong bond of mutual sorrow, one that strengthened the work they did together. June learned from this experience that the company of fellow sufferers in times of anguish can lighten the load and strengthen relationship.

Soon her daughter, Judy, moved back to Chicago to live with June and go to college. Judy was relaxed and energetic, all traces of her illness gone. "We spent a lot of time repairing our relationship and the damage done by my not protecting her enough from her father's inordinate demands. I don't think there could have been a more understanding, loving relationship than what we came to have."

June, forty-six years old, returned once more to graduate school to complete her doctorate in psychology. She and her daughter worked grueling schedules to earn enough to support themselves and attend school. Although this was a physically and emotionally demanding period, it was especially satisfying because June was gaining confidence on all levels—in her own stamina, her professional development, her role as mother, and her identity as a Jungian analyst.

Judy eventually graduated with honors and a fellowship to do graduate work in linguistics at Stanford University. There she met Michael, another linguistics graduate student, who became her fiancé. Shortly after they married, the two of them traveled to Romania, where Michael had a State Department scholarship to study the Rumanian language. June had developed a full private practice by this time and was beginning to gather people to form a new Jungian society in Chicago.

In her interview with me, June recalled a dream that she

had had in Zurich, one that had impressed her with its clarity, but had seemed uninterpretable at the time she had it. Looking back it seemed prophetic. The dream: "I walked into the doorway of a room in our Zurich apartment, and there I saw in the far corner of the room Judy and Richard in bed together with an unearthly light shining over them. I wanted to go in, but Richard threw a solid object in my direction and said, 'You cannot enter here.' It was as though they were in another place, a place I could not go."

Five years after Richard's death, Judy and her new husband were killed instantly in an automobile crash on a lonely mountain road in Romania. When Judy joined her father in death, the loss shattered June's life. Her family had dissolved, and she felt truly bereft.

When the official memorial service, held in Philadelphia, was over, June returned to Chicago and had her own memorial service for Judy at home, with friends, colleagues, and clients. "Judy's death was both a very private and a very public experience. Everybody knew about it in the Chicago Jungian community. Can you imagine what it was like to repeat the story to an endless number of people who would ask tenderly, How do you make sense of this?"

Judy's death was the major turning point in June's life, a wrenching personal sacrifice. The transformation that awaited June was a change in her own attitude, a letting go of a cherished way of seeing things. When June tries to identify what helped her most to move through the stages of transformation—from her initial confrontation with her own pain in Zurich to the ultimate sacrifice of her vision of a lifelong close relationship with her daughter—she says: "There must be an Intelligence in the universe far superior to human intelligence. It has a purpose of its own and a comprehension of the unity of all that is. We don't understand it, but we get glimpses of it, at the level of our personal awareness. The very fact that we can sit here and breathe and make these funny sounds called *words*, and understand from them what's going on inside each other, is an enormous miracle. It is nothing any of us could design. It's clearly not a random thing, but it's also not that God is watching us and making specific events work out one way or another. The Intelligence behind all of this isn't obvious, but it's totally evident if you observe what is happening all around you.

"I learned to accept Judy's death as a part of nature. Accidents are a part of nature. And who am I to be exempt from the pain of this world? I have feelings and so I feel sad and miserable over pain, and delighted in joy. If I blunt myself to either, I'm blunted to both. What is hell? What is heaven? Hell is being fully aware of your feelings. Heaven is being fully aware of your feelings."

June expressed her grief over a long period of time, in her personal life and in her writing. "I think that creativity is often generated by misery. So creativity is the alchemy of making art out of suffering—at least, it was that way for me. My own speaking and writing have come directly from my pain. They've included days and nights of exploring, investigating, trying to see how life works and how it can be improved. You don't feel inclined to do that kind of searching if you're smug and self-satisfied."

The author now of six books, including the widely read *Boundaries of the Soul*, June has impressed many with her clarity, wisdom, and self-knowledge in her writing, lecturing, teaching, and practice as a Jungian analyst over the last three decades.

WHOLE AND DEPENDENT

EXPERIENCING YOURSELF as a victim, too weak, unable to choose for yourself, sets you apart from other people. Isolation and alienation can be healed only through reengaging with life and recognizing the universality of suffering. Through interacting with others, listening to them with an open heart and being fully present, you will find the key to overcoming your resistance to change. But changing takes great effort. Saying *yes* to change is one thing. Acting affirmatively and with courage is quite another.

June had entered the training program at the Jung Institute several months after her husband, so his final thesis for graduation was well under way before she had a clear idea of what she would write about. Richard told her that he would undoubtedly be finished before her, and that she should not expect to remain in Zurich to finish. "I had been thinking of writing on William Blake, and determined that I would at least begin, no matter what. I awoke one night and the whole outline of my thesis came to me as in a dream, and I jotted it down on the yellow pad at my bedside. In the morning there it was, and the strange thing is that it was very well organized. It was as though I was in touch with the Intelligence of the universe, as part to whole, and it was moving through me. I finished the thesis with unusual speed, well within our time constraints. It became the basis for my first published book."

Following through from her dream to write her thesis was a step toward wholeness. June was beginning to feel her own agency, her self-determination and initiative, directly, instead of assuming that they came via permission of Richard (or Mother). She was also feeling her relationship to a source beyond her ego functions, something that "came to her" as a dream does.

Sometimes the idea of wholeness sounds obscure or abstract, but it actually means the ability to draw on a larger context, both within oneself (in terms of trusting both conscious and unconscious coherence) and in relationship to others who sustain us.

June puts it this way: "I have a great belief in wholeness. It's not even a belief, it's a knowledge that individuals and this entire universe have a natural coherence, as opposed to chaos. Our task is to awaken ourselves and others to that coherence. I don't mean helping others in a patronizing way, but to lay out before people the possibilities and offer them the opportunity to recognize what's going on. Many will disregard this, won't care about it, won't appreciate it, but there will always be those who are open and will learn from close attention to the natural order of things."

Learning from this coherence, we move out of isolation. Acknowledging my pain, I can become appreciative of and compassionate about the pain of others. Acknowledging my dependence—on other people and on an Intelligence greater than mine—I feel grateful and connected to a secure "home base," something that sustains me beyond my own self and ego functions. Our strong Western beliefs in the individual soul, hero, genius, have tended to obscure our dependence on others.

But we are in fact always depending on a whole fabric of people and other living beings and things. All beings, from our family members to our neighbors, to the countless animals and insects and microorganisms, as well as the unknown guy on the street who gives us directions, contribute to our biosphere. If we retain a felt consciousness of these connections, we might find it easier to let go of a rigid sense of me and mine. We're never really alone, and our basic emotions and desires are known the world over by other human beings. We're not unique, nor are we isolated. When we feel the pain or suffering of separateness, it is always supported by a belief in being a stranger.

The confidence in feeling oneself as a part of an interwoven fabric of life can be enormous. According to the writer and scholar Anne Klein, who has studied Tibetan Buddhism for years, the Tibetans—although much poorer and less educated (by Western standards) than ourselves—do not know what low self-esteem is. When it was described to the Dalai Lama, he was deeply puzzled because he could not imagine it. Of the Tibetans, Klein says: "They are rarely, if ever, alone in the sense a Westerner in an apartment in a city to which she has just moved . . . is alone. . . . No matter how isolated, even high in a solitary cave, one remains part of a community. . . ."

As I entered middle age, my early life formula (self) of pushing myself relentlessly through every new life experience—travel, marriage, children, divorce, more education, remarriage, greater financial and professional responsibilities—broke down with the inevitabilities of aging. Two chronic illnesses forced me to change and to struggle against my resistant grandiosity: the belief that I had limitless physical energy. Through my illnesses I discovered a principle that has aided me in work and in life. I call it the principle of "absolute dependence"—our constant dependence on others. Similar to Dan, I became aware of my dependence in a completely visceral way when I needed physical and emotional support through my illness. Most of us fend off the knowledge of our dependence in the unconscious belief that we're better off not noticing. Psychotherapy often changes that.

Most people collide full force with the principle of absolute dependence in the course of therapy as they feel their dependence on me, or at least what they take to be their dependence on me. In this kind of "dependent transference," in which people feel that their very lives depend on me, what's actually being felt is the power of something that I represent in my role as therapist (either by virtue of the role itself or the specifics of trust a client has placed in me). The dependent transference may be the first conscious experience of the power of a transcendent coherence, the belief that one will find meaning and purpose in life. The way I see it, people transfer that power to me and then gradually awaken to the transcendent character of it, as therapy ends—or sometime later.

Whole and Dependent

When we alleviate someone's suffering or pain, there's a recognition of connection to this transcendent coherence. This is why compassion, suffering-with, is so powerful. It is an experience of our connection to others and the universe.

A couple of years after his accident, Dan Gottlieb learned to drive a specially designed wheelchair van, which is his magic chariot, allowing him freedom and the feeling of being a regular guy. "After I started driving, I had trouble paying my tolls. I was clumsy and I would drop the quarter. Yet I was very self-conscious and still struggling to be independent. I went over this toll bridge from New Jersey and I'm fumbling to get the quarter in the cup, worried that all these people behind me are going to blow their horns. A toll taker saw me and came over. 'Can I help?' he asked. 'No, I'm okay.' The message was I'm fine, leave me alone.

"I finally get my hand out and throw the quarter and I miss it. It hits the street. I feel like a failure. So I say to him, 'I'm going to need your help after all.' He says, 'No problem,' and puts up his hand to doff his hat—except he had no hand. We smiled at each other. We knew. We knew about being different and about suffering. And aloneness. And that's what I teach and what I want others to see."

Acknowledging pain, alleviating the suffering of others, we start to feel and see our dependence. Intrigued by the world of others, we discover a creative dialogue through pain and suffering, and this allows us to surrender our isolation and our insistence on an independent self.

When compassion is thwarted in our development— either temporarily or chronically—we can become encased in negative emotions and very protective of ourselves.

Despair, resentment, envy, and self-pity are what I call the "apocalyptic emotions" of self-protection. They are signals of disruption of the possibility to discover coherence and meaning through pain and compassion.

About the purpose of pain and suffering, June Singer says: "Our purpose is to find meaning in it. When we find it, there is a kind of mystical connection between what we know and our own sense of purpose. You have to be in proper relationship with the world in order to discover your purpose here, but when that happens you can enhance the meaning of the world and also be enlarged by your purpose."

To find this purpose we have to leave behind a sense of self-importance, the kind that comes from feeling special in our grandiosity or our victimhood. The apocalyptic emotions—despair, resentment, envy, and self-pity—interfere with our discovery of meaningful compassion and enlarge our self-importance.

Despair is the loss of hope and trust and confidence. At its extreme, it is sometimes expressed through suicide. Rather than permit an old self to die, a person literally kills the apparent requirement to change—life itself. Less violent forms of despair involve withdrawing and withholding, turning aggression against the self and acting as though nothing matters anymore. Others are then regarded with antipathy or disdain, and felt connections with humanity are broken. Despair may result from or lead to resentment, depending on circumstances.

Resentment is bitterness arising from hurt held onto over time. A feeling of insult and contempt replaces the desire to connect with others, to share one's help or hurts. Resentment disrupts love and sustenance as the resentful person feels that anything offered is "not enough" to soothe the wound. The woman client I spoke about earlier, whose mother had died in childbirth, was filled with resentment at the beginning of her therapy with me. Nothing offered by family and friends could soothe her hurt. The bitterness of the hurt had replaced any trust in relationships. Resentment often goes hand in hand with envy.

Envy is a form of hatred based on feeling empty of resources that are desired or needed. It is the desire to destroy the resources of another because they can never be imagined to be possessed by oneself. The envious person feels incapable of ever having those resources—like good health or a beautiful appearance—and so believes that the only way to even the score is to destroy, belittle, or demean the envied other(s). If I envy someone for good looks or money, I will hate her for what I imagine she has that I cannot have. I may spend a lot of time putting her down and denigrating her strengths, especially the ones I envy. Some people murder in envy; if they cannot possess what is desired, then they must eliminate the possibility of anyone else possessing it. While envy is a dangerous emotion that always has a destructive effect, self-pity is an insipid one that can become a total barrier to development.

Self-pity is a corruption of compassion and sympathy for oneself. Feeling sorry for yourself focuses attention on what hurts, what is missing. It generates suffering and negativity. Dan Gottlieb felt enormously sorry for himself when he realized that he would never again dance, golf, stroll, stride, or do many of the things that the old Dan took for granted.

Only when he let the old Dan die did he begin to recognize the resources that the new Dan, the quadriplegic, actually had available. Self-pity collapses our feelings in on themselves and we become entangled in our own suffering like a fly caught in a web. The only way out is to recognize that when we let go of our expectations and wishes—of our old self—then we'll discover something new.

The four apocalyptic emotions of self-protection cannot lead anywhere useful or good. They entrap us in egocentric ruminations and prevent us from seeing the meaning of our pain and suffering. And yet they still have value. Many times people seek psychotherapy or similar help when they find themselves trapped in these emotions. They know, or their friends have told them, that ordinary supportive friendship no longer works. They've become too self-enclosed. Perhaps we could say that the important function of these negative emotions is to wake us up in hell, to help us look into the mirror and see who has been giving us so much trouble.

It is when we alleviate suffering—especially the sense of being isolated and incomplete—that we can endure pain. Pain itself, although demanding of energy, is livable and often transformative. When June Singer talks about her own development over a lifetime, she regards her purpose as having evolved from her discoveries through pain and suffering. "I've always felt that it isn't enough to see something and understand it for yourself. It may have personal value, but you discover that its value increases when you share it. Unless it's communicated, you haven't given it the greatest chance of being meaningful. I was so deeply grateful to people who shared with me and guided me without asking anything for themselves. Now I see my purpose in being here as nourishing others, not necessarily in a direct way, but to nurture the unconscious conditions for development by planting seeds deep underground."

Because, as humans, we are capable of great consciousness (although still limited), we have the capacity to change our existence fundamentally, to shape it and color it. More than other life forms, we have choices—about how we live, how we see ourselves and others, and what we take to be meaningful. When we incorporate our pain as meaningful, include others in an understanding of ourselves as fluid and dependent, and reach out in compassion, we inevitably achieve the coherence of inner and outer life called wholeness.

To transform the self, to let it die, and incorporate a whole new identity is to know and embrace a nonessential self—one that is willy-nilly metamorphizing over time. We suffer when we cling to a True Self or demand that life should meet us in a particular way. A crisis, great pain, or confrontation with physical death can shake us out of our habitual attitudes and demand that we change. In this way there is a paradoxical relationship between death and life: to engage wholly with life, we must die many times.

PART FIVE

An Ethic of Suffering

It should be clearly noted that the Buddha did not maintain that all that happens to a person is karmic. He called that belief "karmic determinism" and strongly criticized and rejected it. . . . [T]he law of karma . . . was only one of the laws of nature.

DHARMASIRI, 1989

NOT EVERYTHING that happens to us is of our own making, our responsibility. It is a long and difficult lesson to see the boundaries and domain of our responsibility, how we can and cannot change our lives as we interact with others and the environment around us. But there is a lesson in alleviating our own and others' suffering as we come to recognize how and why we create difficulty for ourselves and evoke negative responses from others.

Joanna Macy has frequently spoken against certain "spiritual tendencies"—especially among people drawn to Eastern religions or New Age philosophy—to think solipsistically, as though *everything* were based on one's own feelings, reactions, actions. She stresses that we do not create our world unilaterally. Although our subjective thoughts can develop into material actions and forms, there is also a "world out there," a world over which we have limited control at a personal level. It is certainly one of the pitfalls of grandiosity to believe that you can control your fate or protect yourself from catastrophe by holding certain values, having a particular lifestyle, meditating, doing good deeds, and so on.

But where is the boundary between our own subjectivity—our thoughts, feelings, perceptions, and actions—and this world of genuine otherness? From the perspective of Buddhist psychology, the distinction is between our own will and attitudes, and what we could call "natural processes"—such as aging and dying—that are beyond our immediate control. Similarly, Jung talks about the difference between neurosis and authentic pain. Neurosis arises from the ways in which we are constantly dissatisfied and full of childish complaints. Authentic pain is beyond our control. It is at the essence of human experience: birth, development, decline and death, and all of the accompanying losses and griefs.

The psychoanalyst Roy Schafer talks about the goal of analytic psychotherapy as the effective recognition of the boundary between personal responsibility and those events over which we have (as adults) or had (as children) little or no actual control. On one hand, a client discovers how she or he has been fragmenting or splitting the emotional world into "good" and "bad"—identifying with one side while projecting the other onto other people or circumstances. The client also sees how he or she has been arranging life to be a series of sexual, social, occupational, financial, or creative failures or traumas. These are matters of personal life and subjective responses. Increasingly, over the course of treatment, the client claims responsibility for the actions and thoughts and wishes involved in creating an emotional world.

On the other hand, the client sees gradually how he or she has been irrationally claiming responsibility for fortunate and unfortunate "happenings" (as Schafer terms them, to distinguish them from actions under the control of a person). Happenings may include major illnesses and physical defects, accidents, early parental neglect and abuse, and deaths and other losses, as well as special advantages, privileges, and opportunities into which one was born. All children feel more powerful than they actually are; they have a grand sense of control in their egocentric way, believing that they singly create the grounds both for joy and for catastrophe in their elders.

As we develop into adulthood, we gain the capacity to think abstractly about our experiences, tracing causal lines from our thoughts, feelings, and intentions to our actions, and from our actions to their consequences. We can look back at childhood and see that magical thinking—the belief that we directly influence other people (making them thrive or fail, for example) or the physical environment (bringing about certain weather or making "accidents" happen) through our wishes and fantasies—is erroneous. We also see that other people don't *cause* us to have feelings or experiences, but that we create those for ourselves.

By the time we reach adulthood, we all have the capacity to review cause and effect in ourselves, but many people do not use this reflective capacity to see how they create many of the conditions of their lives. Instead they simply remain bound to unconscious impulses and emotions and images that are enacted as psychological complexes. Many of us do not know how to take responsibility for our inner lives, and so we feel driven by our childhood complexes, alternating between the roles of victim and aggressor. Yet we each have the capacity to change this. Knowledge of our subjective lives frees us from bondage to our impulses and allows us to direct our compassion and awareness in ways that alleviate suffering for ourselves and others.

A woman in midlife, divorced with two teenage children, schedules her first session of psychotherapy because she's "depressed and overwhelmed, unable to see the point of my life." She complains about her children's lack of respect for her, her own inability to meet her job and financial responsibilities (often feeling overworked and underpaid), and her ex-husband's unwillingness to carry his responsibilities for child care and support. She also has some chronic physical complaints: premenstrual syndrome (or "premenstrual meanies," as she terms it), a tendency to overeat, and occasional migraine headaches. She lives with her thirteen-year-old son and sixteen-year-old daughter in one side of a duplex in a suburban neighborhood outside of Philadelphia. Both of her children have some social and emotional problems in school, but she is more worried about her son, who is frequently negative and critical of her.

She first describes herself and her situation in terms of what "parts of herself" want to do: "A part of me just wants to run away, just leave all this hassle and bullshit to my husband, but another part of me—I think it's the child part—just wants somebody to give me a long hug so I could cry," and so on. A part of her recognizes that she has responsibilities as a parent, a part of her wants to find another man to lean on, and a part of her feels proud that she has managed for three years on her own without falling totally apart. None of these parts is in the driver's seat, and she feels passive and defeated in her everyday dealings. She believes that there's a better life "out there somewhere," but she doesn't know how to reach it.

In describing the reasons for her current difficulties, she relates stories about her mother's depressions and withdrawals, about her traveling-salesman father who "drank too much and probably ran around with other women," about her professionally successful ex-husband who has never been close to his children, and about a heartless boss at her bookkeeping job. The only ways she implicates herself in her hapless story is through "problems with low self-esteem" and "a tendency to give in to other people's needs and not see my own."

Let's call her "Marge" and reflect for a moment on her pain and suffering. There is no doubt that the stresses and unfairness of Marge's single-parenting situation are painful. Probably some of her health and psychological problems are directly related to an overstressed immune system and the emotional hazards of coping with two often-negative, critical teenagers without a support system in the community or family. But the main themes of Marge's suffering—depression and anxiety—are rooted in expectations and ideals for how life should be.

She looks back on her marriage to "George." Although George had seemed mostly motivated by the admiration and achievements linked to his practice of law in a prestigious firm, he had brought many comforts and privileges to Marge. She had grown used to living in a roomy suburban home, surrounded by well-kept grass and gardens. She had liked her own part-time work coupled with homemaking. The "picture of me in a gracious home with two wonderful children" had been the picture in Marge's mind of what her adult life would be. Marge had never pictured herself working full-time, living in a duplex with two teenage children, divorced with no partner in sight.

George had not fit into her picture of a happy, close family, though. He had become increasingly preoccupied with work, and she felt his withdrawal from the family as a coldness and lack of devotion. She had been angry and then aggressive in response—accusing him of being a "workaholic" and blaming him for much that went wrong in the family. Now that their marriage had ended, Marge could not "get a new picture" of what her life was to be. She felt distressed, afraid, irritated, and aggrieved that her expectations for herself and her life were not being met. Her children seemed "a disappointment" and her job was "more and more demanding with less autonomy."

If I listened only to Marge's words, I would feel hopeless. I would catch her contagious depression and believe she wasn't a candidate for psychotherapy because her problems were overwhelming her on multiple fronts. I might want to refer her for antidepressants before even trying psychotherapy. I might collude with her self-portrait as a victim unable to make a difference in her chaotic, dissatisfying life. Marge described herself mostly in terms of circumstances under the control of others. When she gave the litany of the different parts of herself, I could sense her paralysis. A "part" cannot act. It can only observe and react.

Instead of simply accepting her account, I looked at the

conditions from which Marge was suffering in terms of the pictures she created of her world. I could see how those pictures could evoke problematic and unsupportive reactions from others.

In presenting and portraying a victim self, Marge probably irritated and angered her children, who felt that she should be in charge of her life. She was an adult, after all, and they were children. Her friends and her coworkers might feel sorry for Marge, encouraging her to expand her self-confidence and notice her strengths—functions that Marge had never developed for herself, leaving them up to others. Marge *never* felt good enough about herself to claim directly her own capacities.

Her ex-husband probably responded to her complaints by withdrawing and stonewalling; he tried to shield himself from the shame and guilt she stirred up in him. He found it hard even to meet with her to discuss their children's welfare.

Her boss, in trying to help Marge by giving her extra tasks at work to increase her income, probably felt double-crossed when Marge complained about his overworking her, because she had repeatedly told him that she needed to make more money.

Marge was always generating images of herself as not having or being "enough." She didn't have enough time or money. She didn't get enough respect or support. Her achievements and capabilities weren't good enough, and so on. Her old self—a privileged gracious homemaker—had to die, but Marge wouldn't let it go. She had come close to living her "ideal life," but then the only problem had been

George: he wasn't home enough. Yet when she "got rid of him," the whole picture shifted.

IN DOING JUNGIAN ANALYSIS and psychotherapy for thousands of hours, alongside thousands of hours of Dialogue Therapy for couples, I have had a wide and rich opportunity to observe the struggles of taking personal responsibility for our lives. The key factor is to recognize that we create many of our own problems.

The Buddha termed this karma, a natural principle of cause and effect. The theory of karma in Buddhism is distinct from predetermination, which is more related to Hinduism. The Buddha stressed that the principle of cause and effect is not predetermined, but rather a fluid process of ongoing creation. At any instance, at any moment of reflection, we can change our life and our destiny. Our suffering—as we've repeatedly seen—is largely the product of our own expectations and ideals, holding onto a particular picture or outcome for ourselves. Even if we are already caught up in a pattern of difficult circumstances, as Marge is, we can find a new perspective, a way to lessen suffering. That is why the old Chinese sage rides his mule backwards; he's paying attention to his own attitudes because this is where his responsibility lies.

The resilient have shown us distinctly that meaning is created in each new context; it is not a given. When the little girl Shibvon was being sexually abused by her mother's lover, she saw herself as helping her younger siblings by keeping the perpetrator's attentions on her. When Dan

Gottlieb was in pain and humiliation, with a Halo vest bolted to his skull, he became aware of how his pain opened him to others and how his life's purpose was to teach others about alienation. Neither Shibvon nor Dan could do much about their circumstances, but they could transform their attitudes and find meaning that would convert their pain into compassion and help for others. This is the difference between hell and heaven as we recognize that our own responses, our attitudes, are the powerful lenses of reality in the ways in which we affect others and evoke responses from them.

Similar to present-day psychoanalysts, the Buddha emphasized not only the consequences of actions themselves but the consequences of our motivations. The Buddha used the term karma specifically referring to volition, the intention or motive behind an action. He said that the motivation behind the action determines the karmic fruit. "Inherent in each intention in the mind is an energy powerful enough to bring about subsequent results." As we reflect on Marge's situation, we see that she unknowingly brings about negative results for herself by unintentionally enacting the victim, believing that she does not have *enough* of this or that to engage fully in her life.

Marge re-created a situation with me (through her transference and my responses to it) in which she felt I would never be able to really meet her needs. She frequently asked me to change appointment times, to do her special favors by lowering my fee or lending her my books, or to talk to her about some fairly trivial matters on the phone outside of our appointed meetings. If I refused, declined, or even hesitated to do this, she would feel rejected and left out. If I fulfilled her request, she was not especially grateful, but treated my generosity as though it was to be expected because her need was so overwhelming. When I declined to do a special favor, she would say, "You're just like my father and my ex-husband; you always have some *reason* why you can't do what I need." At this point she would withdraw from me and threaten to leave the therapy. Essentially, she would refuse to make use of what was available.

Marge's responsibility lay in her unconscious motive of presenting herself to others in terms of the theme of not-enough. Unknowingly, she identified with her depressed mother, who had played out a drama of martyrdom and self-pity that had deeply affected Marge in childhood.

Although Marge was often angry with her mother's passivity and negativity in childhood, as an adult Marge was unconsciously playing out a negative mother complex. Essentially, Marge was re-creating her mother's life and evoking from George and others (like her therapist) a negative emotional reaction, the desire to take flight from Marge's needs. When Marge engaged in the drama of not-enough, she didn't validate or appreciate what was available to her. Instead, those around her would feel "invisible" and "unknown"—just as Marge had felt as a child of her mother.

In Marge's negative transference to me as the father/husband who could not meet her "simplest needs," she gradually awakened to the meaning of her karma, the actions and attitudes she had been generating in the drama of not-enough.

Transcendent Function

No one can save us from our own unconscious tendencies but ourselves. In knowing that complexes arise in us, rather than being forced on us by others or the world, we can begin to experiment with stepping back from their influence, with changing our minds. Then, when we look into the mirror of self-recognition, we no longer see ourselves as passive victims of things "happening to me." This is similar to the Buddhist notion of seeing oneself as the source and cause of a hellish existence. Although the hand holding the mirror is actually one's own, it can appear to be that of one's therapist, a partner, or one's child.

When we see ourselves as the agents of our own suffering, it is no longer important to say, "My mind is playing tricks on me" or "My anger exploded" or "Being a woman has ruined my life"—passive complaints that one has no responsibility or opportunity to change. Instead one says, "I have been confused from time to time" or "I was angry and retaliated" or "my own attitude about my sexuality and gender has been a problem." Engaging actively with one's subjective life means literally feeling how powerful one is in having an attitude, a point of view.

Consciously claiming our complicity in creating our own suffering, we begin also to have access to our inner lives. We see how we impose our assumptions and meanings—both grand and fearful—on what happens to us, on what we do and what is done to us. Resisting our tendencies to defend our complexes, we develop an ability that Jung called the "transcendent function." It is the capacity to hold tensions and let a meaning emerge without prematurely deciding whether a situation is "good" or "bad."

This capacity is well illustrated by an old Chinese story frequently quoted by Roshi Philip Kapleau: One day a farmer lost his horse because it ran off and his neighbors came to console him, saying "Too bad, too bad." The farmer responded, "Maybe." The next day the horse returned, bringing with him seven wild horses. "Oh, how lucky you are!" his neighbors exclaimed. "Maybe," the man responded. On the following day, when the farmer's son tried to ride one of the new horses, he was thrown and broke his leg. "How awful!" cried the neighbors. "Maybe," the farmer answered. The next day soldiers came to conscript the young men of the village, but the farmer's son wasn't taken because his leg was broken. "How wonderful for you!" said the neighbors. "Maybe," said the farmer.

Meanings emerge over time, not in events themselves, and through our perspective and actions we make the events purposeful and fulfilling or empty and distressing. From the perspective of the transcendent function, we cannot say that Dan's breaking his neck was only "bad" or that my growing up in a discordant household was primarily a "loss of child-hood" or that Joanna Macy's encounter with a tyrannical father was entirely "tragic." All of these events are both difficult and rewarding when seen from a larger perspective of compassion and development.

When we allow meaning and possibility to emerge, we begin to feel freer and calmer, as long as we acknowledge and accept our limitations. We do not unilaterally control how anything turns out, and so we can never "get it right." Our control resides in our own subjectivity—our attitudes, decisions, emotional life. The Buddhist idea of "dissolving negative karma" refers to an ability to transform a negative complex, something that is re-created out of emotionally driven dissatisfactions, into compassion and new meaning.

As we have seen, the resilient are able to do this first through helping others and then through letting an old self die. They are able to create a fluid identity that is responsive to new troubles and suffering. It isn't that they have found a way to live without pain and adversity, to transform every event into happiness. Rather, they have learned how to make use of pain and adversity in expanding their knowledge and compassion.

Looking at experiences on the scale of everyday life, how do we make these moments of resilience available to ourselves? Of course, as the hermit says to the emperor in the earlier story, they are always present in the situations and people around us. We don't need to go somewhere or do something special to find the transcendent function, the ability to hold tension without premature judgments. We need only pay attention to our tendencies to thrust ourselves into despair or grandiosity, to act impulsively and to create dukkha. When problems arise, whether as trivial as a traffic jam or as traumatic as a divorce, we can practice the transcendent function by creating a "space" in which we wait for meaning to emerge rather than impose our own discontent.

Other psychoanalytic terms for the transcendent function may be helpful in fleshing it out so that you can grasp its importance. From Donald Winnicott, a psychoanalyst and pediatrician, we have inherited the term "potential space" or "play space" for the ability to wait for meaning to emerge. Winnicott describes this attitude as the origin of all true creativity. It is the ability to hold a frame around an experience and to play with its meaning, not to engage immediately in the idea that it means this or it means that. Only when we await a discovery and keep ourselves from imposing old meanings do we actually encounter something new. Many everyday challenges provoke reactions that may create more suffering or be an opportunity for growth and discovery.

A common challenge for maintaining potential space is conversation between life partners—spouses or other partners—in which there is a tendency to repeat familiar themes. When conversations feel dead, partners are reiterating their old points and demanding to have the floor or be heard. Or perhaps one partner withdraws and "lets" the other one speak in a vacuum. There is a palpable feeling of power struggle, and nothing new is discovered. If you examine the assumptions of the partners, you'll find some version of psychological complexes, usually the victim and the aggressor, being played out by both. The specifics of the drama would probably be different for each, having come through different families, but the overall effect of feeling caught or driven would be the same for both people.

Because conversation is a two-way street, a "system" made of both people's parts, only one person would need to find the potential space, or the transcendent function, in order for the dynamic to change and the possibility for creative discovery to emerge. If one partner stopped indulging an old complex and began to hold the tension, to look at the events through a "maybe" perspective, then both people would be freed up to have a true dialogue, an exchange of discovery. Too often we're waiting for the other person to change rather than looking into the mirror of self-recognition to see how we might change.

When tensions can be examined playfully with the spirit of discovery, we begin to regard our suffering as useful for self-awareness and development. Then we hold the middle way between the extremes, and don't take ourselves deadly seriously, and we can tap into the creative power of archetypes as images of powerful emotional states, rather than enact them blindly. This is the outcome of truly creative tension. If there is no discovery in our tensions, then we have missed the transcendent function and the possibility for play.

Dialogue Therapy, a form of couples therapy originated by my husband and me that I described in detail in two of my previous books, was designed to facilitate the transcendent function and the development of potential space in long-term committed relationships. Combining Jung's psychology with other psychodynamic theories, this method enhances the ability to hold tensions during conflict and to wait for new discoveries to arise through dialogue.

Many partners fall into acting like helpless children or

punitive parents in their interactions with each other, although they may feel free of this negative karma in other relationships. Instead of gratitude and respect for their dependence on each other, they are drawn into despair, resentment, envy, and self-pity. In place of trust and development, the relationship is filled with suffering and bitterness.

When people retain a potential space and allow for the transcendent function, they protect their relationship from being the scene of negative karmic enactments, the repetitions of primitive emotional patterns from early family life. Feeling grateful for their mutual dependence, they promote new discovery by asking questions, listening carefully, paraphrasing, and respecting differences. This kind of attitude engenders the possibility that conflicts will be opportunities to discover something new, as two people keep themselves from becoming aggressive or indifferent to each other. This doesn't mean that conflict or intense emotions are eliminated. It means that they are handled with respect for the transcendent coherence, or deep connectedness, of the partners.

Although this attitude is related to a meditative awareness, it is different because there is a specific goal in the transcendent function—to discover a new solution, a new insight, a compromise, or a new synthesis. It is a way of seeing into our conflicts in order to move beyond them, just a bit, to a new way of understanding, something that had been previously unknown.

When the transcendent function is used in relation to oneself, it is a matter of opening up the space between our thoughts and not moving compulsively from one thought or image to another. Meditation certainly enhances the awareness of this space, but so does the capacity for sustained self-reflection of the kind that can be developed in psychotherapy and in some educational contexts.

The psychoanalyst Thomas Ogden describes this as recognizing the "dialogical space" in ourselves. It's the "space between" a symbol (a word or expression or gesture) and an experience (that which is being symbolized through the word or gesture). In that space we remain alert to the fact that there is a *person* who is creating a response to an event. The response is not creating the person. The response is not automatic, concrete, or given. Ogden sees one goal of our development in adult life to be the acute awareness of this subjective factor in our own thoughts, reactions, and images—our point of view. He doesn't mean constant self-consciousness or awareness of oneself, but rather the felt freedom to look at things from many different angles because one realizes that one has only a point of view, not a God's eye view. A deep humility comes with this awareness, as we come to value others' views as much as our own.

Looked at from the starkest place, we could say that we never "discover" meaning, that we always "invent" it. And yet our experiences are not purely subjective; they are not arbitrary or imagined. We are all embodied in the same form and constrained by its limitations. Many of our experiences—like our perceptions of the physical world—are human, shared, fundamentally consensual, and yet accented or colored by different emotional and cultural lenses. Joanna Macy has written, "Perception . . . is a highly interpretive process. We create our worlds, but we do not do so unilaterally, for consciousness is colored by that on which it feeds; subject and object are interdependent. . . ."

Knowing our responsibility for our thoughts and feelings, while holding the tension of a conflict or a conflicted moment within ourselves, we can move beyond our habits, our complexes, and our immediate suffering into discovery and development. This is the means by which we surrender an old self in a time of crisis as much as it is the way we can step outside the tired, old assumptions of embattlement with a spouse or partner. Strangely enough, this ability to hold tension and be aware of our own assumptions and expectations often leads to a lessening of self-consciousness as we learn to let go of self-protective emotions.

KARMIC GROWING PAINS

WHEN PHILIP KAPLEAU began his serious Zen training, in 1953, at a monastery in a cold area of Japan, he submitted willingly to excruciating pain. Trying one sitting position after another, nothing would ease the fierce pain in his legs, and "yet I couldn't quit. I wouldn't quit. As bad luck—or should I say 'bad' karma—would have it, rain began to fall and the weather turned cold. Next to pain, cold was my worst antagonist. It was December and there was not a bit of heat in the zendo (meditation hall). The rain, the absence of sun, and the cold—all these added to my misery." On the third day of this ordeal, his spirits were picked up by the sun breaking through, and so Kapleau threw his whole being into the struggle, ultimately fainting and toppling off the rickety chair that he had been generously offered (probably the only chair the monastery could find) as a concession to his having had no experience sitting in the normal cross-legged or kneeling postures for meditation.

Later in the same seven-day retreat, the intensity of challenge increased as Kapleau was prodded all night long by a senior monitor who was intent on Kapleau's being able to "break through" into greater consciousness. When Roshi Kapleau looks back on these first years in Japan, he asks, "What motivated me to subject myself to such harsh training and, more importantly, persist in it for the three years I trained at Hosshin-ji?" And he responds, "The answer is simple: I stayed because I needed the treatment given me. At a deep level of my being I knew that, given my karma, only through this kind of tough training could I hope to begin to dissolve the oversized lump of ego I called myself. So I take no credit for what I did. I never was, nor am I now, any sort of iron man. The fact is, I was 'on the road I knew not of, going to a place I knew not where.'"

Philip Kapleau remained in Japan for thirteen years to train under two distinguished masters of Zen Buddhism. When he returned to the United States in 1966, he had been sanctioned as a Zen teacher by Yasutani-roshi, one of the greatest living Zen masters of that period (he died in 1973). While in Japan, Kapleau wrote what would be the Zen Bible for many young Americans attracted to Buddhism, *The Three Pillars of Zen*. Translated into twelve languages, it remains a great classic and, for many, the book that has opened the way to practicing Zen Buddhism.

Although it may appear that Roshi Kapleau chose this challenge of pain and discipline, whereas others like Dan Gottlieb have endured their challenges accidentally, we often have little immediate or personal control over the major events of our lives.

Our karma, the effects or consequences of our actions and attitudes, will draw us inexorably into the conditions that provide just what we need to awaken to greater compassion and consciousness, if we don't resist too strongly. Resistance is usually based on the wish to be in control, on the fantasy that we can be. The wish to control sets us apart from others and makes us feel exempt from the fluctuations of life. When June Singer began her personal analysis in Zurich, she faced a great resistance in herself; she experienced herself as lacking in enough self-confidence to make her own choices.

Roshi and June had two very different experiences of resistance to change and development, and yet they each epitomize a common kind of difficulty. Roshi described himself in terms of an "oversized" ego, a certain attitude of superiority or cynicism. June described herself as unable to know what she was thinking and feeling, as being too inhibited to express herself. Both of them (in their resistance to change and greater consciousness) held onto an identity that separated them from others and left them feeling adrift.

Roshi's early development led to a certain kind of isolation and cynicism, a bitterness about human relationships, that was the product of the family situation into which he was born. Philip Kapleau—the fifth of the six Kapleau children—was born in New Haven, Connecticut, in 1912 into a family already strained under poverty and marital discord. There was to be a fifteen-year period during which Philip was the youngest child, until another brother, unwelcome by his mother, was born. The birth of her youngest child brought out the worst despair in his mother, who resented the child, born so late and conceived with a man for whom she had no love. "My mother taught her children to dislike their father. I had no love for either parent, no real love. I recall my mother saying, 'When you grow up, don't forget how badly you and I were treated by your father and be sure to make him pay for it.'"

Young Kapleau found little comfort or warmth in his early family life. "My parents were constantly quarreling. As a child, I could only feel resentful about my mother's 'attacks' on my father. She would always tell us that he was lazy, and complained that he wouldn't work, though he was a skilled tailor. We were on welfare a lot and she blamed my father for that. After my youngest brother came along, things got even worse. She constantly referred to him as her 'affliction' and clearly rejected him. I felt she was being so unfair to him; after all, he didn't ask to be born. (This stance I later changed when I began my study of Buddhism.)" It's no surprise that Kapleau eventually felt self-protective and cynical about family relationships. Having developed a negative mother complex, he had difficulty trusting being vulnerable or relying on others for sustenance. "In the end," he says, "I rejected both parents and the God they vaguely believed in."

Kapleau's mother was Jewish, and his father was Eastern Orthodox. Early on, Kapleau was intrigued by religion as a way of discovering what the struggle of life was about. He went to many churches, trying to find one that might have answers that he could believe. As Roshi realizes now, the rabbis and priests and ministers he had heard in childhood had no intimate experience of the God they spoke about. And so their sermons seemed lifeless and dry. By the time he was sixteen, he was so disillusioned with Judeo-Christian religion that he formed the Atheists' Club in his high school, serving as its president.

After he graduated from high school, having lost his savings (from doing odd jobs with his brothers) in the 1929 stock market crash, Kapleau went to secretarial school. "I was lucky enough to learn shorthand and typing. So I got a job in the Works Progress Administration in the office of the Administrator for the state of Connecticut. It was a secretarial job." Although he had earlier been interested in becoming a lawyer, young Kapleau decided to become a court reporter instead.

He moved from the city court to the common pleas court to the superior court of the state of Connecticut. "There is nothing so dreadful as a certain kind of court trial: a family fight over property or a contested divorce. In such cases the worst things come out in people, the hatred and bitterness." Kapleau's feelings were especially intense about such courtroom battles because his experiences in court reinforced a defensive self-protectiveness as he repeatedly saw what he had witnessed in his mother: people's unwillingness to take any responsibility for the misery they created and their insistent blame of others.

Philip Kapleau was almost thirty years old at the time of Pearl Harbor, but because of a medical deferment he did not go to the war in Europe until he was commissioned to a post at the Nuremberg trials of the major war criminals in 1945 as the chief court reporter. The contrast between the decadent life he witnessed in postwar Nuremberg and the hideous evidence of the concentration camps was further indication of a profound lack of conscience in humanity.

Kapleau was shocked and devastated by what he heard, but ultimately he felt numb. "So many thousands burned at such and such a place and so many thousands killed in another place. After a while, your mind can't register the details or grasp the enormity of such crimes. I suppose it's a survival mechanism. You just can't think about this kind of thing in detail." The defendants were always squabbling and complaining, especially complaining that they were being tried as criminals. "They believed that their actions had been protected by the fact that there was a war under way. They constantly insisted that other countries, the very countries trying them, had fought unjust wars. Why should they now be treated as criminals when they had simply been serving their military?" Kapleau was aghast that no one would take responsibility for the atrocities committed during the war.

At the end of his tenure at the Nuremberg Trial A, Kapleau applied for a transfer to serve as a court reporter for the International Military Tribunal for the Far East in Tokyo, Japan. When Kapleau arrived at the trials in Tokyo, he was immediately struck by a very different emotional tone from that of Germany. The trials of these major war criminals were more civil and relaxed. The defendants were allowed American as well as Japanese counsel. And "we could say 'Good morning' to them, a gesture forbidden at the tense Nuremberg trials." People were friendly to each other, including the officials at the trial, and there were respect and congeniality among the prosecutors.

In Japan, as in Germany, there seemed to be a great ignorance among ordinary people of the heinous crimes of the military elite, especially the infamous "rape of Nanking" in China, which began when the Japanese troops landed in Shanghai and began destroying civilian and cultural monuments "because the Chinese would not surrender. Soldiers just cut people to pieces with bayonets and raped and murdered everywhere. This went on for one week straight. There were awful atrocities—and no mention of this in any Japanese history books." But despite the ignorance of the general populace, there was an acknowledgment in some quarters that the Japanese had done serious wrong to their enemies. One could hear ordinary people say that the great miseries of Hiroshima and the bombing of Japan were retribution, negative karma, for the atrocities of the Japanese. But most Japanese still felt that none of their atrocities equaled the atrocities of Hiroshima and Nagasaki.

While at the trials, Kapleau met the eminent Buddhist scholar D. T. Suzuki and an American student of philosophy, Richard DeMartino, who had come to Japan as a historian at the trials for the Defense Department. At the time, Kapleau had no particular interest in Buddhism. "I didn't even know who Suzuki was. A Japanese employee at the trials who was trying to curry favor with me told me, 'He's a world-famous philosopher, and if you would like to meet him, I can arrange it.'" So Kapleau told his friend DeMartino, who recognized Suzuki's name at once. "DeMartino and I would go over to Suzuki's small house in the monastery compound to meet with Suzuki from time to time. I knew nothing about Buddhism. Suzuki would give a lengthy talk, but I was more interested in the aesthetics of the monastery. It was a very beautiful place. The quietness and the magnificent trees brought me back again and again."

Kapleau attended other lectures on Buddhism, but found them "over my head. I read a little, but I didn't understand the philosophy. Nonetheless I saw something that was quite understandable and profound. The average Japanese took responsibility, at least verbally, for the war crimes of Japan, while the average German refused to take any. When the Japanese talked about how severely Japan had been bombed, they'd say, 'Well, this is our karma. We did terrible things to others and now we have to pay.' A lot of this was probably not sincere, but some of it was, and you'd hear it often. Although Japan had been heavily bombed and the Japanese were really suffering from the bombing, their attitude was, verbally at least, good—they willingly took responsibility." The Germans, on the other hand, would always say, "Why did you Americans bomb us so ferociously? What did we do to you?" More than anything else it was this willingness of the Japanese to take responsibility for their negative karma that attracted Kapleau to Buddhism. Here was a religion that offered the hope of transcending his own bitterness and isolation. That Buddhism promised a coherence between human action and its consequences was enormously inviting.

After the court verdicts were announced, Kapleau was invited to stay for subsequent trials, but he declined and returned to the United States after making his first ever trip to China. Back in Connecticut, he developed a freelance business and "finally decided that I would go to Columbia University to study with D. T. Suzuki" who had been invited to lecture there.

In his classes at Columbia, Suzuki was teaching the religion and philosophy of Buddhism (with no mention of meditation). Among Kapleau's classmates was the musician and composer John Cage. Kapleau audited classes taught by theologian Paul Tillich, and met the psychoanalyst Erich

Fromm, the poet Allen Ginsberg, the psychoanalyst Karen Horney and many of the "West Coast beatniks." Kapleau also enrolled in a class for psychiatrists and psychoanalysts that Dr. Suzuki was teaching. There were many intensely stirring moments in these classes, and Kapleau felt himself drawn more and more into an interest in religion. He studied Christianity and Hinduism at Union Theological Seminary, but at a certain moment decided that "this was like force-feeding baked bread"—it was already sifted material. "So in 1953, I sold my business, my car, and my apartment and everything in it, and I returned to Japan."

He studied initially with English-speaking Soen Naka-gawa-roshi at Ryutaku-ji Monastery and then, on a recommendation by Soen-roshi, was welcomed by the prominent Zen master Daium Harada-roshi to train at his monastery in the cold climate of northern Japan. Despite the overall warm welcome that Kapleau received from his teachers, he was "shocked and dumbfounded" by the reality of monastic life, so different from what he read about Zen in Dr. Suzuki's books. All the same, he spent three years in severe and demanding conditions at Hosshin-ji Monastery with Harada-roshi. These were difficult years for Kapleau's health: unheated rooms, a spartan diet, and severely demanding meditational retreats were the norm. He was forty-one years old when he returned to Japan.

He continued his Zen training for ten more years under Yasutani-roshi, and was ordained by him as a Buddhist priest and later given permission to teach. While in Japan, he married a Canadian woman, Joan deLancey Robinson, and they had a daughter in 1960. In Japan he also began to work on *The Three Pillars of Zen*. With the encouragement of his teacher, the book took shape as a bridge between the needs of Western practitioners and the demands of authentic formal training in Japanese Zen.

When Kapleau finally returned to the United States, in 1965, "I'd thought I'd settle down in sunny California or someplace like that, but my karma decreed differently. I got this invitation to teach at Rochester, New York, from Dorris and Chester Carlson (he was the inventor of xerography). So I spent most of my adult life in a gray northern city that wasn't unlike—at least in regard to climate—that at the site of the Hosshin-ji Monastery."

Roshi Kapleau founded the Rochester Zen Center in 1965. His work in the United States has included teaching and writing both here and abroad. He is the author of five books on Zen Buddhism. He has also founded other Zen centers in Canada, Mexico, Costa Rica, Poland, Germany, Sweden, and a dozen other cities in the United States.

When I asked Roshi how he thought that suffering and pain contribute to transformation he said: "There's no doubt that suffering is a pathway to the spiritual. I think that's the reason why so many people in this country are turning to Buddhism right now. We face so much pain and suffering with violence and mindless killings in our society. Buddhism can help us understand how to face this situation and continue to be engaged in our lives."

When I met Roshi Kapleau for this interview, he was recovering from minor surgery. At the age of eighty-three, Kapleau has a mild form of Parkinson's disease and some other chronic problems, but to all appearances he maintains a demanding schedule of Zen practice, lectures, retreats, exercise, and advice-giving.

I have the deepest love and respect for Roshi Kapleau, who is my own Buddhist teacher. In his pursuit of knowledge and wisdom, he is serious and funny, thorough, scholarly and iconoclastic. His manner and physical appearance are sprightly, vulnerable, commanding, powerful. He is powerful in a vulnerable way, and although that may be paradoxical, it is exactly the case. Although now fragile from age and illness, Roshi exudes freshness and life—something like a small whirlwind, calm at the center.

The particular configuration in his childhood that shadowed a lot of his adult life, and may have presaged the transformative response to suffering that Roshi experienced at the war crimes trials, was his mother's hatred of his father and rejection of his younger brother. Witnessing unlovingness and acrimony and cruelty in childhood, young Kapleau tried to distance himself from the conditions of familial relationships because of their apparent hypocrisy. Encountering similar conditions in the courts, and their epitome at Nuremberg, Kapleau felt his suffering ripen into cynicism. But on finding and practicing Buddhism, Roshi came to terms with this karma. Eventually he developed compassion for his mother, too. Roshi says: "I came to realize that she had a side too. It was tough for her at forty-seven to have a child by a man she didn't even love. And I also realized that the Buddha said, 'We are not, as many suppose, born through the will of our parents. Rather, rebirth has as its basis our karma and as its propelling force the desire for rebirth.' So we all ask to be reborn and are drawn to someone from whom we can learn what we need to know. So my younger brother has his responsibility too."

In the course of Roshi's life, then, his suffering led from early empathy for his younger brother and for his father, and criticism of his mother, to later cynicism and bitterness. This cynicism was the resistance surrounding and protecting the "oversized lump of ego" that Kapleau mentioned above. Roshi's karma, the consequences of his intentions and actions, led eventually to his encounter with Buddhism. Intensive Zen discipline and practice allowed him to break through his resistance and eventually to awaken to the true nature of our existence. But this was not the end; in a sense it was only the beginning. In his ongoing confrontation with adversity, in his own and others' lives, Roshi expresses tireless creativity and compassionate action through his teaching and writing and practice. Through his practice of Buddhism, Roshi always has access to a transcendent function that allows him to hold the tension of conflict and wait for meaning to emerge.

NEGATIVE EMOTIONS

JUST AS ROSHI had to recognize and overcome his cynicism and bitterness, all of us must battle the desire to protect ourselves and resist the notion that we're responsible for our suffering.

Traps of self-consciousness, feeling unique or special whether in a positive or negative way, are barriers to engaging directly with our lives. As we've learned, pride, shame, envy, guilt, embarrassment, and jealousy are emotions born of body boundaries, of feeling oneself as an individual being. These self-conscious emotions are problematic both in developing meaningful compassion and in the process of taking responsibility for one's own thoughts, feelings, actions. When we strongly identify with any of them, in times of stress, loss, or crisis, the intensity and combination of pain and suffering will often seem too great to overcome. Our energy and focus will simultaneously be bound to self-assessments and comparisons with others, in addition to being taken up with the actual pain or difficulty of the loss.

Emotion, as I use the term, is a condition of human life that is inescapable: a patterned response of motivation and expression that connects us to our animal roots. Emotions are organizing functions, inborn to predispose us to certain actions in certain situations. Physiologically, negative and positive emotions are often indistinguishable: they are both arousal systems. But psychologically, some emotions are frequent barriers to personal responsibility.

Earlier I described envy as one of the apocalyptic emotions of self-protection. Here I'll go into more detail, because envy is also an insidious barrier to responsibility and self-awareness, and often signals a serious defensiveness against engaging directly in one's life.

Envy develops out of the initial experience of separateness of self and other, perceiving the other as having more resources than the self. It is expressed in the desire to *destroy* what another possesses because one cannot possess it for oneself. Different from jealousy, which is the coveting or desire to *possess* what belongs to another, envy is a form of hatred that is deeply destructive. Jealousy can lead to positive actions of wanting to be competent and trying to compete with others, but envy always has the effect of destroying something, never of sustaining it.

The first step out of envy is to recognize that one is feeling it. Often this is difficult, because it means acknowledging that one feels empty in some important area of life. Take, for instance, the envy that some infertile women may feel for other women who are having babies. Rather than focusing on their own bodies and feelings, these women can feel an irrational hatred of pregnant women. No amount of rational explanations will "cure" the hateful feelings toward others. Identifying with envy, infertile women might say,

"Being pregnant is the only thing that could help my feelings right now." The envy has been concretized into the belief that only an actual baby could fill the void created by envy itself.

The recognition that one *feels* empty, rather than that one *is* empty—is an effective way to begin to free oneself of envy. Seeing that empty feelings arise in the self and are promoted by assumptions that one is left out of the human circle, one can move on to look at what is being idealized as the "baby" in this case.

Things are never as concrete as they seem to be. Babies, material possessions, lovers, education, and even development are weighted with fantasies and expectations about what they'll bring us. For us to recover from envy, these fantasies have to be examined and known so that we can move more consciously to fulfill ourselves. In the case of maternal envy, a woman may find that the "baby" symbolizes something she otherwise has or can develop—like the capacity to nurture another or to develop herself or to know that her love is good.

After recognizing one's envy, one must acknowledge the resources that actually exist in the self, although they may not be identical with those that are envied. To recover from envy does not mean to deny it, but rather not to identify with it and make it into a permanent state of being. Instead of believing that one is left out, or that one lacks what is necessary, we notice that the feeling of envy arises under certain circumstances (where we feel a lack) and then it fades. It arises with self-consciousness and comparison, and it fades with gratitude for what we have. Feeling grateful for the resources that we actually possess, and seeing our potential for developing them, connects us with our own lives and moves us beyond envy. No one can feel both envious and grateful at the same time. (Of course, gratitude is transitory too.)

What about shame? Shame is a popular emotion these days. Contemporary psychologists, of both the pop and the serious varieties, have offered up many accounts and interpretations of shame. Some of these confuse shame and guilt, in my view. Shame is a negative assessment of the whole self, whereas guilt is a negative assessment of a particular action. Shame is global and guilt is local, so to speak. Shame leads to wanting to hide or disappear or die, whereas guilt leads to the desire to make reparation. When we feel ashamed of something, it usually thwarts our capacity to feel guilty because the shame will lead us to cover, abscond, deceive.

The other side of shame is pride, the confident display of the self. When shame is simply compensated, but not made conscious, it can turn into pride and an eagerness to boast. A cycle of shame and pride is a painful suffering that leads to power struggles about who is "on top" and who is not.

So called "shame-based" psychopathologies—from addictions to personality disorders—are connected to identification with shame and pride. They are marked by a tendency to hide and disguise faults and shortcomings while being haunted by them under the surface.

The major first step for alleviating shame is, again, to recognize that one is feeling it. A second step—that can be taken in psychotherapy or through some discipline of self-awareness—is to see how we hold onto self-protectiveness through identifying with shame or pride. This tendency to hold onto "I" or "mine" usually grows from the desire to control resources and protect the self. Self has become a "thing," a piece of territory that must be defended.

As we saw earlier, from a Buddhist perspective, this tendency arises in ignorance of the no-self, in our conviction that our self-protective feelings are necessary to defend "something." Jung claims our self-protectiveness is most dominant when we feel least connected with others and least conscious of what motivates us. When self-conscious emotions arise, they tempt us to feel discrete and alienated. Because individuality and uniqueness are highly valued in our society, too often we fall into feelings of specialness and exemption that may have either positive or negative origins. Then we begin to create in ourselves and evoke from others the "evidence" that we are set apart.

While envy, shame, and pride may tempt us to create and sustain an experience of being alien or separate from others, two primary emotions—fear and aggression—can motivate us to treat others as enemies. In taking responsibility for our own subjective responses, we need to become aware of how these two emotions can be problematic and how they are different from anger, an emotion that can assist us in handling conflicts with respect for self and other.

I have said very little about the anger and retaliation people are often inclined to express when hardship befalls them. There have been so many wrongheaded approaches to "getting out your anger" coming from the advice of American psychotherapists over these past decades that I often hesitate to take up the topic unless I'm asked a direct question.

Too many people in our society have what the psychologist Carol Tavris calls a "ventilationist" bias. They believe that "getting out" their negative feelings is somehow honest, healthy, and/or justified. As Tavris suggests in her book about anger, openly expressing negative reactions is usually not the best course to take, from the perspective of ongoing relationships or one's own peace of mind.

And yet I want to distinguish between two kinds of negative responses and their consequences: one that I call "aggression" and another that I call "anger." I believe that anger is a useful emotion to recognize in oneself and can be useful to express. *Anger*, as I use the term, is a "moral emotion" (as the Greeks called it). It's the experience of indignant and hostile or retaliatory feeling in response to some perceived injustice. It always involves reflection (because how could you otherwise know that something seems unjust?), and is never an attack on someone or something else. It's not a knee-jerk reaction as aggression is.

When humans get angry, we have a choice of whether or not we want to express it because we can reflect on the bigger picture and see if we're likely to right the wrong that has been done. People can express their anger at the present moment through words, or in the future through plans to do something creative with it—hold a demonstration, make a painting, clean out a closet, or write a letter. At other times there is no place to direct our anger. Anger then may transform into resentment and must be examined in the mirror of self-recognition. Anger is not a fight or flight reaction, but involves holding tensions well enough to reflect about what is taking place.

Sometimes anger can change the world, when it is expressed in a way that is likely to be heard and understood, or when it is expressed symbolically in a timeless way that will endure. The civil rights movement was a memorable such moment in our recent history in which anger was expressed through symbolic means and used to transform an unjust system toward greater justice. Movies and works of art and books are created as timeless expressions of anger. The point of expressing anger is to change an unfairness, to respond to an injustice done to oneself or others.

In conversation, anger sets boundaries. It is expressed either in terms that are direct such as "I'm angry about . . ." or in ways that fix a limit or set a constraint. Saying "Don't" or "Stop" or "I don't like that" are all expressions of anger: clarifying what one is able and willing to tolerate. Without that knowledge, other people may intrude in a way that is unnecessarily painful to all involved. Anger can save us energy and trouble when it is expressed in a way that stops something from going too far or in a wrong direction.

The way I use the term "aggression" distinguishes it from anger. Aggression is an instinctual response to fear or dread. It is aimed at protecting the self, often by attacking another or withdrawing from another. Aggression may be expressed as "fight" or "flight." The "fight" kind of aggression—active aggression—involves attack (physical or emotional), intimidation, name-calling, blaming, trivializing, or negatively analyzing another person. Exploding in one's rage or hostility or attacking a physical object (hitting a wall, for instance) is aggressive.

The "flight" kind of aggression—passive aggression—

involves withdrawal, stonewalling, procrastinating, using humor self-defensively to put down another, and turning aggression against the self (putting yourself down). When aggression is expressed, whether in conversation or war, it will encourage more aggression or fear. Aggression does not settle anything, because it is inherently frightening. When a person behaves aggressively, others become afraid and tend to behave aggressively in response.

Often the fight type of active aggression, when expressed in conversation, will evoke the flight type of passive aggression. One person is screaming epithets and the other is covering her ears or walking away.

When aggression is expressed openly in response to pain and suffering, it evokes more pain. This is a simple demonstration of karma. If you respond to your suffering or pain by attacking someone else (or the environment, by destroying something), then you are likely to have more pain because you will "evoke" it. When the samurai raised his sword over the monk in the story of heaven and hell, the samurai was creating hell. When a nation or a person reacts in an aggressive manner, it creates a condition that promotes an atmosphere of fear, self-protection, and more aggression.

If you can be calm and reflective at a moment of great difficulty, you can begin to determine whether there has been an injustice or whether you are reacting out of a complex of self-protectiveness or grandiosity. If you find that you yourself are the problem, then you can step back and recognize it. But if you determine that an injustice has been done to you or another, you can use anger to express the grievance. Anger is effective as a communication for setting limits and responding to injustice. It is a statement about the self and the domain of one's tolerance, but it is not an attack on another.

When aggression is openly expressed in response to a conflict, it is destructive to our connection to others. The principle of absolute dependence, that we're all more dependent than otherwise, is an important deterrent to expressing aggression. Although I'm not by any means perfect in containing my own aggression, I've promised myself that I'll use anger, not aggression, when necessary in a conflict because fundamentally I know that when I've attacked or diminished another, I've attacked or diminished myself.

When fear or aggression or anger passes through us and is simply recognized as such, then we don't need to worry about it further. It is merely a passing response or reaction. Only when it lingers and infects our thoughts and actions do we have to take the steps outlined above. Our anger and fear can be communicated and integrated into the larger context on which we depend. In this way we sustain the connection by responding honestly without aggression.

REBIRTH

There is no self that is reborn; there is an ongoing continuity of "again-becoming." In each moment of life the individual is born and dies, yet he continues. The same is true of the moment of death.

PHILIP KAPLEAU, 1989

To DISCUSS THE ETHIC of suffering, karma or responsibility, without including rebirth would be a mistake. From a psychological perspective, we encounter death and rebirth many times throughout what we regard as a lifespan. When we cling too tightly to an old self, or to our personal expectations of what a new self should bring us in the way of advantages, then we are doomed to suffer greatly.

But if we can release ourselves into a new existence as life demands it, we continue to grow and develop, to garner the lessons that are made available. These lessons come through our compassionate responses to our and others' suffering, through our increased self-awareness and willingness to take responsibility for our actions and intentions.

Too many times in psychotherapy I have encountered the suicidal desires and wishes of a client who is deeply, profoundly ashamed of living in her or his condition. Such a person often feels afraid to engage in the life she or he has created because that life seems so permanently flawed as to be impossible to retrieve. When I say "too many times," I mean that our society offers little wisdom about how to contend with life's difficulties and not despair when we have either personally failed or been burdened by miseries that seem to come from the world around, our biology, sexual orientation, gender, race, or class. Far too often people commit suicide out of the mere wish for release.

What is this wish? As I've explored it with many people, it is usually a magical thought that death equals disappearance, falling asleep forever, going out of the universe. Death then seems to be the perfect answer to shame, and the ultimate release from responsibility.

This belief that we disappear in death is in many ways the product of a certain scientific way of thinking: for something to be true it must be demonstrated empirically. The assumption here is that empirical truths are final, that they go beyond interpretation. This account of truth has played a major role in the scientific myth of our period. Although it has been revealed as inadequate by another account of truth—that claims human interpretation *cannot* be transcended and that all we know is colored by it—the empirical account still tends to be persuasive in a large segment of Western culture.

A particular version of scientific empiricism is known as "rational empiricism." Its main working hypothesis about human life is "What you see is what you get." That hypothesis has been translated into the belief that death is a disappearing act. If death is the end of the physical body, then what you get from it is only an ending. That's it. If you can't see any more than that, then nothing more is going on.

This scientific minimyth about death provides a handy rationalization for suicide if someone is profoundly ashamed, and for homicide if one is profoundly envious. Like other kinds of magical or omnipotent fantasy (that we control things by our wishes and will), the story of "What you see is what you get" seems to me to be far too simple-minded. Death has been an unsolvable mystery for eons of time, and belief in an afterlife has persisted in human cultures all over the world. It seems to me that "What you see is what you get" is just too small a plot for death.

I think it would behoove us to reexamine any notion that we have arrived at the final truth about death through rational empiricism. Otherwise, we sound as though we have stepped way outside the human circle in making concrete claims about what happens after death. Our philosophers may not speak for all of us, but the philosopher Thomas Nagel says very confidently what I've heard too often from clients seriously contemplating suicide:

> Some people believe in an afterlife. I do not; what I say will be based on the assumption that death is nothing, and final. I believe there is little to be said for it: it is a great curse, and if we truly face it nothing can make it palatable. . . .

I'm not a metaphysician or theologian. My concerns are the practical ones of a psychologist and the transcendent ones of an ordinary human being. From a practical position, knowing what I do about theories of human development (that are solidly grounded in empirical science), I see no reason to conclude that death is final. As an ordinary human being I have not seen beyond death in any way, nor have I remembered any previous lives or had any other form of omniscience. And yet I can imagine death only as a transition, as a part of life in its continual transformation of energy and form.

So when people come to me with wishes to disappear in death, I always ask first "What do you believe you'll gain by killing yourself?" and I've always heard the kind of response recounted above. No one has ever said "Rebirth" or anything close to it. It has always been the disappearing act that is the goal of suicide. Then I pose another question: "What if death is merely a continuation of life and suicide is likely to make things even more confusing and difficult than they are now—having to deal with all the feelings that you'll stir up in violently doing yourself in?"

Usually the wishful thinking evaporates with this question. The listener considers, often for the first time, the possibility that death is development, a transition, that needs to be prepared for and encountered naturally. In my clinical experience, not one person seeking suicide has thought about death as a transition rather than a disappearance. When people have contemplated death as development, whether they are young or old, they have ultimately wanted to reengage the life they are living and find some way to face confusion and difficulty in their current embodiment.

When I talk to suicidal clients, I often say: "What if this life you're living was designed *especially* for you? Containing certain lessons that are not arbitrary, but quite personal? Would you be interested in continuing it until you could discover those lessons?" Often the answer is yes.

Increasingly, as I've worked as a therapist, I've appreciated the law of cause and effect that our actions and intentions bring outcomes that are inescapable. In Buddhism, the karma from a particular lifetime leads also to a rebirth in a next lifetime that reflects the on-going consequences of thought and action. There is no way to avoid or evade the lessons before one. They will carry over to a next existence, as karma moves from action to consequence. The conditions into which one was born, that will mark one throughout a lifetime, are specific opportunities and dynamics of development connected to previous lifetimes. Roshi Kapleau puts it this way:

> We are here to work out past karma, both positive and negative—a statement which has a much broader implication than that of paying off past karmic debts. You can think of our present life as a huge school or arena where we seek to develop ourselves physically, mentally, morally, and spiritually—in other words, to raise the level of our own consciousness and the consciousness of others.

The thought that each lifetime is a "huge school" resonates with what I've seen in clinical work with people of all varieties of health and illness. We can see this through an account of involuntary pain such as Dan Gottlieb's, as much as we can in a transformative path that seems to be chosen, such as Roshi Kapleau's. In both cases, their positive and negative karma pushed and pulled them into discovering purpose, self-awareness, compassion; only their resistance interfered and caused a lot of suffering.

From a Buddhist perspective, there is a coherence or logic to an individual lifetime. Buddhism teaches that we are "attracted" or compelled to be born to our specific parents. In other words, that we got the parents we did is not arbitrary. Our psychological complexes are shaped by the conditions of the family we're born into. Those complexes, propelled by strong emotions, motivate us to re-create patterns of relationship and identity that tend to re-create the original patterns into which we were born. Through these childhood complexes, we're attracted and repelled toward or away from certain kinds of people and life situations.

Over the life span, then, either we are doomed to "repetition compulsions" (as Freud referred to them) of our early relational and identity patterns or we gradually wake up to free ourselves through consciousness. At each new stage of development, as we change our physical and cognitive and emotional capacities, we have new opportunities to break through into greater consciousness.

This knowledge has allowed me to walk with people through some rather confusing and messy territory until we could make sense out of their psychological complexes, seeing what the causes were and how they've been re-creating miseries, until finally they were able to stop reenacting them.

At that point a freedom emerges—the freedom to see oneself and others in the context of larger purposes. The great spiritual questions about the purpose and meaning of life, the basis of truth and reality, and the nature of death inevitably arise spontaneously after a person has begun to get free of the grip of childhood complexes. It is as though we cannot see into the larger context of human meaning until we can shake ourselves out of our narcissistic and traumatic wounds and biases—at least enough to see behind the wall of suffering.

The particular pain and suffering that a person encounters and creates will connect him or her with a particular kind of knowledge and compassion. As we saw in the accounts of four lives, the suffering arising from psychological complexes—our neuroses or disturbances—is often the first opening we have into deep curiosity about what is going on around and within us. Suffering leads to questions about meaning and purpose in life. Pain, loss, and limitation awaken us to the problem of a separate self, how we feel cut off and alienated and cheated. These conditions, coupled with some experience of love (given or received), provide opportunities for us to improve ourselves if we're able to see things from a perspective beyond the separate self and "What you see is what you get." From a Buddhist perspective, it "is precisely the combination of pain and pleasure in the human realm that provides the best circumstances for deep understanding and realization."

As witnessed in the life stories presented here, we have seen how death and rebirth take place within the life span. Although there is profound change in the patterns and motives of an individual, something carries over from old self to new self. That "something" could be called an integrative function, the function of continuity and coherence through self-image and perceptions. From the perspective of Buddhism this same kind of something carries over after the death of the physical body. It is described as a configuration or dynamic that has developed from the actions, motivations, and desires—the karma—of an individual. Just as you are not the same person you were at birth, you will not be the same person at rebirth that you'll be at death. The karma from an individual life goes through some predictable transformations during the death-to-rebirth process, but the capacities of free will and consciousness are considerably reduced during this rebirth process. Opportunities to change karmic patterns are more accessible during the conscious lifetime than at any other stage, according to testimonies and records of Buddhist scholars and teachers. Human life is considered to be a precious opportunity for development and liberation.

By observing yourself in your own life, you'll come to see a lot about how you create and re-create suffering until you can understand your responsibility in it and step back from it. Looking back over the different personalities and capacities that you've been and had in even a decade, you'll see that life is characterized by change and impermanence, although something has seemed unchanging. In understanding that you are not the same self you were ten years ago, you can begin to see what Buddhism teaches about the transitory nature of self. In seeing how you've played out your own childhood emotional patterns, you'll see something about what Buddhism says of karma and what Jung and Freud have said about the compulsion to repeat the patterns from our pasts until we become conscious of them. You can probably see also how your own interests, knowledge, work, and relationships are expressions (in some way) of what you've gained or understood through suffering.

AN ETHIC OF SUFFERING

This is the character of human life that propels each of us into opportunities for development. Although we may resent the pain and hate those whom we blame for it, we cannot learn about ourselves without it. In contemplating our own lives through this lens, it is easy to recognize the logic of rebirth. The logic is simply that death is not the end, but a transformation similar to the many transformations we can easily remember.

I call this a psychological understanding of the principle of rebirth—and I believe it is a stronger hypothesis from a rational perspective than the hypothesis that death is the absolute end of our development. In any case, the hypothesis of rebirth assists me greatly in helping people make sense of their psychological complexes. Because I believe that there is reason in our initial life circumstances, that our fate is an expression of a principled universe in which we developed over eons of time, I can be more objective about accepting and discovering meaning in childhood trauma, losses, disabilities, illness, and even death.

Feeling the coherence of a purposeful universe helps me understand more, not less, about the scientific discoveries of our period of time, especially in developmental psychology and the study of human consciousness. Perhaps more than anything else, this felt coherence increases my compassion and courage in encounters with human karma, our actions on all levels of existence.

PART SIX

Lessons

Zen master Dogen has pointed out that anxiety, when accepted, is the driving force to enlightenment in that it lays bare the human dilemma at the same time that it ignites our desire to break out of it.

PHILIP KAPLEAU, 1969

THERE IS A DEARTH of methods and theories about how suffering can be useful in the contemporary world. Coming from the elite ranks of medicine, biology, and sometimes even psychology is an almost uniform lack of interest in the value of suffering. Instead the focus is on avoiding or eliminating it. This strategy tends to increase our worst fears—that pain and suffering are intolerable and useless. I've told a different story here, an alternative way of looking at our hardships as major catalysts for change and development.

I'm writing against the current tide that includes a widespread assortment of recovery and New Age formulas for how to stay healthy, happy, and in control, as well as the hard-core scientific ideologies of genetic engineering that promise us cures for all major diseases and the possibility of conquering death. Trying to find a gene for criminality, a physical cause for hopelessness, and ever better drugs to treat our negative moods, we direct our gaze toward nature to locate the origin or cause of our suffering. This is a grave error.

Much of our suffering originates with our own discontent. When we discover that, we begin to find a path to freedom. Our society is moving in a psychologically and spiritually dangerous direction, as we attempt to explain more and more of our personal difficulties through biology and genes. We've dropped the mirror of self-recognition.

Without the capacity to see how we create a lot of our own difficulties, we are morally and spiritually adrift. We are often deeply perplexed about the increase in violence and destruction in our cities and the willingness of our young people to take their own and others' lives, but it is obvious that there is no widespread understanding of the ethic of suffering: that one is the creator of oneself and that whatever we do, we become heir to our actions. There is no felt personal connection between actions and consequences, no belief that death is a transition, no hunger for compassion or service as a means to self-knowledge.

A famous story about the Buddha tells of his encounter with a teenage mother who has lost her infant to death. She is frantic with grief and outrage and has traveled from village to village, carrying her child on her hip, looking for a miracle that could bring the child back to life. Someone tells her that only the Buddha, who is preaching in a nearby town, would be capable of such a miracle. When she arrives at the town and finds the crowds around the Buddha, she pushes her way through and stands before him.

"If you would perform a miracle and bring my child back to life, I would do anything in return," she says with touching sincerity. The Buddha sees the depth of her grief and says, "If you bring me a mustard seed from a home in which there has been no death, then I will perform the miracle." This sounds like a small task and she readily agrees, setting off with the deepest gratitude in her heart.

She travels from door to door in this and other villages, carrying her dead child and asking at each house if there has ever been a death. She hears about many difficult deaths and much disease and her heart is opened to other people's pain. Eventually she realizes that all families have been touched by death and she returns to the Buddha.

"I know now what you were trying to teach me," she says. "I am not alone in my misery. All people must endure death, not only their own, but others around them." The Buddha gently offers to perform a funeral for her child and then to teach her how suffering can be alleviated. Thus she becomes one of his most dedicated followers and eventually a powerful teacher in her own right.

As we have seen throughout this book, the only real freedom from suffering and death is to accept them, to be interested and begin to see how they connect us to ourselves through meaning, and to others through compassion. Although we may find many cures for illnesses and some relief for pain, only when we can transform our own fears and anxiety into interest and curiosity do we have access to the knowledge and compassion that give life purpose. This sense of purpose brings greater creativity and transcendent coherence, allowing us to move more smoothly through future difficulties and losses, appreciating the riches they provide in the context of the demands they make on us.

Yet today we have little interest in how to make sense of suffering, maintaining instead a sometimes singular focus on how to quell the pain that can teach us so much. There is a tendency now to assume that depression is a "biological disease" because we have antidepressant medication that sometimes works well to relieve symptoms. There may well be a biological component to some depressions that might even have psychological origins, but we have in no way empirically demonstrated that depression is a biological disease. Biochemists don't even know why antidepressant drugs work to alleviate some depressions. And yet we make claims that we know what depression is and that we have defeated it.

Depression is still a transitory mood, one that we all have from time to time, and we don't know much more about its origins than we did a hundred years ago. We know something about some kinds of depression, but we don't know the big picture. The hype surrounding the new antidepressants focuses our gaze on biology, not on our own negativity or discontent.

In his successful book *Listening to Prozac*, the psychiatrist Peter Kramer not only advocates Prozac—or similar SSRI antidepressants, that increase serotonin levels—for most cases of depression, but he claims that it can make people "better than well." Why would anyone want to be better than well? It's one thing to improve a debilitating depression so that a person can awaken basic self-awareness, but it's another to try to escape the ordinary problems of living. Readers of Kramer's book can easily come away with the impression that Prozac will solve life's problems, everything from a bad mood to low self-confidence. Even though anti-depressants *can* help us stabilize a difficult mood disorder, if we look to the medication to solve life's problems, then we've broken the connection between suffering and meaning.

In my experience doing therapy with depressed and anxious adults, I have seen them become resilient within the cycles of depression and renewal by seeing how their own psychological complexes—the negativity and discontent—triggered their depressed moods. Looking into the mirror of self-recognition, we can all reduce the despair, resentment, envy, and self-pity that increasingly characterize many of us living in the affluent societies of today's world.

We need far more opportunities to hear stories of suffering, to explore our own experiences in some meaningful context, to be mentored or guided through the fundamental transitions from suffering to compassion, and to become knowledgeable about the ethic of suffering.

In large measure, we in Western societies have a social problem with "idealization"—a grandiose fantasy about who we are and what we should control—that can separate us from other peoples and other species, and may have already put us at high risk for extinction. This kind of idealization, a tendency to feel exempt from the natural conditions or limitations of human life, stems from illusions of control and independence. Many aspects of Western culture, from our stories of individual heroes and geniuses (stories that always eliminate the influences of family members and others who might have contributed to "greatness") to our beliefs in the True Self, promote isolation and overestimation of our personal worth—perhaps even the worth of our species.

The human ability to think abstractly, to manipulate symbolic concepts apart from concrete situations, is perhaps one of the greatest resources of our species. When it goes unchecked—driven primarily and unknowingly by *dukkha*—it can also lead to ruin, as the desire for greater and greater competence overtakes our experience of interconnection.

Our economic systems are grounded in competition and individualism, and although we have the potential for the complex responsiveness of true democracy (valuing a range of different points of view and responding to a range of needs), we seem more and more to be moving into a zero sum game that focuses on personal stakes (like *my* pocketbook or *my* safety versus yours) and pulls in the direction of self-protection and isolation. Rather than working together to achieve goals that are shaped first and foremost by the interdependence of our needs and those of other life systems, we often end up protecting the most privileged humans. In large part this is the product of believing in individual rights to happiness, no matter the expense to other people and other beings.

Unless we can begin to see that our inherent discontent and drive for increasing competence run up against our interdependence or connectedness, we humans may not survive the next millennium. Our drive for competence may be the great instinctive weakness that topples our species. We can see how negative thinking might have benefited us in the evolutionary process, compelling us to greater and greater manipulation of the environment for our own needs. But from the perspective of the delicate balance of the ecosystem of life, our ever more competent adaptation may be ill suited for the long run.

Our capacity for competence sets us up to feel exempt from the constraints and limitations of life on this planet. But in recognizing our suffering, seeing how we create it, we can free ourselves from the constant press to improve and begin to experience the vast interconnectedness of our existence.

As we develop personal responsibility for our attitudes, intentions, and actions, we begin to free ourselves from the dictates of self-protectiveness. We ride the mule backwards and see ourselves in the mirror of hellish existence. We gain the capacity to transform hell into heaven.

What is so striking about the resilient is how smoothly and quickly they create a coherent and meaningful story from hardship, misery, trauma, abuse. They shape painful, desperate events into unity and purpose, into compassion and creativity. This might seem like some sleight-of-mind trick if we had no conception of how we create worlds from our own attitudes and responses. From psychoanalysis and Buddhism alike, we glean ideas about why our meaning, our attributions and intentions, are so vitally important in shaping a life.

When you change your perception of an event or a person, at that moment the perceived also changes. Subject and object are joined by perception. This account of a world resting on consciousness seems far-flung only if we hold onto the notion of a separate self. When we conceive of the self as wholly interdependent, functioning to integrate and bring coherent image and meaning to diverse perception, then we appreciate more deeply the freedom that human beings have brought to the world. This freedom is one of making new meanings, especially of opening ourselves in times of pain and suffering to the roots of our compassion. When we cross the bridge from self-protectiveness to compassion and knowledge, we have changed the world. Without the ordinary occasion of human suffering—our own discontent—it is likely that we would never find the bridge.

APPENDIX
Interview Format

This interview will explore the effects of difficulty, pain, or suffering on your development, contributions, service, and creativity. I am acquainted with your work. I have chosen to speak with you because of the ways in which you have apparently transformed difficulty or suffering, or witnessing of suffering, into service, compassion, inspiration, creativity, and/or an appreciation of life. Rather than direct this interview from my prior knowledge of you, I would like to hear what you consider to be the difficulty or pain that seems most pivotal in your development. This may be one or several events or conditions. I would like to follow the thread that you believe links this difficulty to later developments and transformations.

The questions listed below are launching points for discussion. I want a basic structure for all my interviews for this project, but within that structure I will follow your lead. I'm giving you the questions in advance so that you know what interests me. Do not feel that you need to prepare in any

way for the interview. I prefer that our meeting be sponta-
neous. Thank you.

1. Please describe the situation(s), event(s), or circumstances that led to the experience of suffering that has been
most transformative, cycling through your life and work in
new and different meanings over time. I'll follow your lead
and ask questions about the experience itself—the shock,
fear, whatever was engendered.

2. What kind of meaning did this situation carry at the
time or near the time of its occurrence? Did anything like
this happen to your family members or friends? How old
were you at the time? How did you initially try to cope with
the situation and/or sustain yourself?

3. If this experience took place in childhood, how did your
parents respond? Your siblings? Other adults or parental
figures (like teachers, a pastor, a relative)? If it took place in
adulthood, were there friends or others with whom you
could share your difficulties or pain? Who were these people? How did they help? Did they also fail to help? What
was most helpful and least helpful about others' responses?

4. How do you think this experience has affected your
personality over time? Are there any aspects that have been
a setback to your development—temporarily or permanently? If it seems that the experience enhanced your development, could you describe how? How do you compare
your life before with your life after this experience?

5. How do you see the beginning of the transformation from pain and suffering into development, service, or inspiration? Please talk about the time framework and the context of meaning as you see them. Were you able to begin a process of transformation immediately, only gradually, after years? What assisted you? What interfered?

6. How do you see the transformation of the event(s) over time? How have they interwoven with your ideas about yourself, others, the world, etc., as these have emerged in your service to others, your own creative work, or any other expression? Please talk about the ways these ideas have changed, if they have.

7. How have friends or community helped or not helped with the development of meaning from these event(s)? Do you have close relationships with a few friends? With many people? How do you see the interface between these relationships and your continuing development from the event(s)?

8. I would like to ask you about your childhood, but your response is not crucial to what I hope to find from the interview. Feel free to decline to answer. I'd like to hear: How would you basically describe your relationships with your parents in childhood? Your siblings?

9. When you were upset as a child and felt afraid, what would you do? How much did you turn to other people, parents, or siblings? How much did you turn to religious or

spiritual comforts or meanings? How do you see the relationship, if any, between what has taken place in your transformation in adulthood and your ways of handling difficulty as a child?

10. What do you want to say to others or even teach them about your experience? How do you see the relationship between difficulty or suffering and development? What are or were the key factors for transformation so that you could go forward with hopefulness and enthusiasm about life?

11. How do you understand your own spiritual development in light of this event or events? Perhaps the term "spiritual" does not seem comfortable to you. If so, could you explain why? How did you form a context of meaning around the circumstances of your difficulty and suffering? What seemed to be most important to you in weaving this context?

NOTES

Page   *Introduction*

3 Jung: The idea of transformation of the "lowest" into the "high-
   est" is expressed throughout Jung's later works, especially after
   1935. For a discussion of this kind of transformation, see C. G.
   Jung, *Alchemical Studies*, vol. 13 of *The Collected Works of C. G. Jung*,
   2d ed., trans. R. F. C. Hull (Princeton, NJ: Princeton University
   Press, 1959), pp. 110–189; Jung, *The Symbolic Life*, vol. 18 of *The
   Collected Works*, 2d ed., pp. 5–182.

                               Part One

5 "old Chinese sage": The detective novel in which my client
   found the story of the old Chinese sage was by E. S. Gardner,
   Case of the Backward Mule (New York: William Morrow, 1946).

7 "antisuffering campaigns": Contemporary North American culture offers many quick-fix solutions to relieve psychic distress.
   For example, antidepressants prescribed to enhance an individual's coping strategies by elevating mood are misrepresented as
   a cure that will erase all that is wrong in a person's life. See
   P. Kramer, *Listening to Prozac: A Psychiatrist Explores Anti-Depressant
   Drugs and the Remaking of the Self* (New York: Penguin Books,
   1994). Jane Hirschmann and Carol Munter point out in *Over-*

coming Overeating (New York: Fawcett Columbine, 1988) that, although decreasing caloric intake changes only a person's physical appearance, most fad diets promise to eliminate not only the extra weight but all attributes people are ashamed of (gluttony, poor relationships).

7 "dysfunctional family": A term popularized in the 1980s. It refers to a family system where at least one parent lacks responsiveness, warmth, stability, and child-oriented parenting skills. The term was first coined to describe the chaotic childhood family environments of adult children of alcoholics.

8 Freud and Jung: The idea that insight can alleviate neurotic symptoms can be found throughout Freud's work, but especially in S. Freud, "Remembering, Repeating, and Working Through," in vol. 12 of *The Standard Edition of the Complete Psychological Works of Sigmund Freud*, 2d ed., ed. J. Strachey (London: Hogarth Press, 1960); this concept is also apparent throughout Jung's work, but it is particularly evident in C. G. Jung, *The Collected Works of C. G. Jung*, 2d ed., vol. 16., trans. R. F. C. Hull (Princeton, NJ: Princeton University Press, 1959).

9 Jung: Jung's idea of "compensation"—in which the conscious or manifest aspects of personality are in tension with their opposites in the unconscious—contains the inherent idea that neurotic symptoms distract us from actual pain. This idea, and its expansion into a larger philosophy about the purpose of neurosis (to awaken us to our own dividedness), is developed throughout *The Collected Works* but found especially in *Two Essays on Analytic Psychology*, in vol. 7, and *The Practice of Psychotherapy*, in vol. 16, of *The Collected Works*, 2d ed.

9 "remain children": See Jung in D. J. Meckel and R. L. Moore (eds.), *Self and Liberation: The Jung-Buddhism Dialogue* (Mahwah, NY: Paulist Press, 1992), p. 50.

10 "Buddhism": The following texts provide an overview of Buddhist religion and philosophy. Dalai Lama, *A Policy of Kindness* (Ithaca, NY: Snow Lion Publications, 1990); J. Goldstein and J. Kornfield, *Seeking the Heart of Wisdom: The Path of Insight Medita-*

tion (Boston: Shambhala, 1987); P. Kapleau, *The Three Pillars of Zen* (New York: Doubleday, 1989); J. Kornfield, *A Path with Heart: A Guide through the Perils and Promises of Spiritual Life* (New York: Bantam Books, 1993); N. W. Ross, *Buddhism: A Way of Life and Thought* (New York: Vintage Books, 1980); W. Rahula, *What the Buddha Taught* (New York: Grove Press, 1974); S. Suzuki, *Zen Mind, Beginner's Mind*, ed. T. Dixon (New York: Weatherhill, 1970).

13 Jung: See Note for p. 9.

16 "the war": I'm referring to World War II.

19 "secure attachments": See E. Erikson, *Childhood and Society* (New York: W. W. Norton, 1950); E. Erikson, *Identity and the Life Cycle* (New York: W. W. Norton, 1980); J. Bowlby, *Attachment*, vol. 1 (New York: Basic Books, 1982); J. Bowlby, *A Secure Base: Parent-Child Attachment and Healthy Human Development* (New York: Basic Books, 1988); D. N. Stern, *The Interpersonal World of the Infant* (New York: Basic Books, 1985). The notion that a difficult childhood leads to an unproductive adulthood is evident in the research that was generated from this perspective: see W. Dennis, *Children of the Creche* (New York: Appleton-Century-Crofts, 1973); H. Harlow, "The Nature of Love," *American Psychologist* 13 (1958): 673–685; H. Harlow, M. K. Harlow, and S. J. Suomi, "From Thought to Therapy: Lessons from a Primate Laboratory," *American Scientist* 59 (1971): 538–549; R. Spitz and K. Wolf, "Anaclitic Depression," *Psychoanalytic Study of the Child* 2 (1946): 313–342; D. W. Winnicott, *Human Nature* (New York: Schocken Books, 1988); and for a review, see L. Yarrow, "Maternal Deprivation: Toward an Empirical and Conceptual Re-Evaluation," *Psychological Bulletin* 58 (1961): 459–490.

20 "advantages of adversity": For a discussion of the theoretical perspective that adversity can yield advantages for development, see C. G. Jung's autobiography, *Memories, Dreams, Reflections* (New York: Random House, 1961); H. S. Sullivan, *The Interpersonal Theory of Psychiatry* (New York: W. W. Norton, 1953); H. Kohut, *The Analysis of the Self* (New York: International

Universities Press, 1971); H. Kohut, *The Restoration of the Self* (New York: International Universities Press, 1977).

20 "resilience": Ann Masten, Karin Best, and Norman Garmezy have identified three uses of the term resilience: (1) good outcome despite high-risk status, (2) sustained competence under threat, and (3) recovery from trauma. See "Resilience and Development: Contributions from the Study of Children Who Overcome Adversity," *Development and Psychopathology* 2 (1990), p. 426. Another researcher represents resilience not as invulnerability but as the least detrimental of all possible outcomes. See S. S. Luther, "Vulnerability and Resilience: A Study of High-Risk Adolescents," *Child Development* 62 (1991): 600–616. Each of these definitions suggests that the resilient may also succumb to adversity. The critical difference is that the "resilient" or "stress-resistant" cope significantly better than expected with adversity.

20 "African American woman": See A. L. Cox, "Childhood Adversity and the Successful, Resilient Black Adult: A Retrospective Qualitative Study" (Ph.D. diss., Smith College School for Social Work, 1994), p. 68.

21 "past fifteen years": The earliest research studies of resilience include M. Bleuler, *The Schizophrenic Disorders: Long-term Patient and Family Studies* (New Haven: Yale University Press, 1978); N. Garmezy, "The Study of Competence in Children at Risk for Severe Psychopathology," in A. E. Koupernick (ed.), *The Child in His Family: Children at Psychiatric Risk* (New York: Wiley, 1974); N. Garmezy, "Observations of Research with Children at Risk for Child and Adult Psychopathology," in M. McMillan and S. Henao (eds.), *Child Psychiatry: Treatment and Research* (New York: Brunner/Mazel, 1978); C. Kaufmann et al., "Superkids: Competent Children of Psychotic Mothers," *American Journal of Psychiatry* 136, no. 11 (1979): 1398–1402; C. E. Vaughn and J. P. Leff, "The Influence of Family and Social Factors on the Course of Psychiatric Illness," *British Journal of Psychiatry* 129 (1976): 125–137.

Notes

Although many unanswered questions concerning resilience remain, the current recognition of the importance of investigating this phenomenon is reflected in the growing number of studies on risk and protective factors in the fields of developmental psychology and developmental psychopathology. See, for example, E. L. Cowen et al., "The Rochester Child Resilience Project: Overview and Summary of First Year Findings," *Development and Psychopathology* 2 (1990): 193–212; R. F. Dugan and R. Coles (eds.), *The Child in Our Times: Studies in the Development of Resiliency* (New York: Brunner/Mazel, 1989); A. S. Masten, K. M. Best, and N. Garmezy, "Resilience and Development: Contributions from the Study of Children Who Overcome Adversity," *Development and Psychopathology* 2 (1990): 425–444; D. O'Grady and J. R. Metz, "Resilience in Children at High Risk for Psychological Disorder," *Journal of Pediatric Psychology* 12, no. 1 (1987): 3–23; J. Rolf, A. S. Masten, D. Cicchetti, K. H. Nuechterlein, and S. Weintraub (eds.), *Risk and Protective Factors in the Development of Psychopathology* (Cambridge, England: Cambridge University Press, 1990). The 1990 volume of the journal of *Development and Psychopathology* was devoted entirely to research on resilience.

22 "The voices of the resilient": See S. B. Fine, "Resilience and Human Adaptability: Who Rises above Adversity?" *American Journal of Occupational Therapy* 45, no. 6 (1991): 493.

22 "resilience is neither a single action": The researcher Michael Rutter points out that resilience is not a set of fixed characteristics. Its presence varies across *and* within individuals. Rutter, like other researchers, hopes that the identification of risk and protective factors will lead to interventions to promote resilience in the majority of individuals. See M. Rutter, "Psychosocial Resilience and Protective Mechanisms," *American Journal of Orthopsychiatry* 57, no. 3 (1987): 316–331. Also see E. J. Anthony and C. Koupernick (eds.), *The Child in His Family*, vol. 2 (New York: Wiley, 1973); A. S. Masten and N. Garmezy, "Risk, Vulnerability, and Protective Factors in Developmental

Psychopathology," in B. B. Lahey and A. E. Kazdin (eds.), *Advances in Clinical Child Psychology,* vol. 8 (New York: Plenum, 1985); M. Rutter, "Psychosocial Resilience and Protective Factors Mechanisms," in J. Rolf, A. S. Masten, D. Cicchetti, K. H. Nuechterlein, and S. Weintraub (eds.), *Risk and Protective Factors in the Development of Psychopathology* (Cambridge, England: Cambridge University Press, 1990), pp. 181–214.

22   "The resilient have returned to life enriched": See, for example, G. O. Higgins, *Resilient Adults* (San Francisco, CA: Jossey-Bass, 1994); R. Krell, "Child Survivors of the Holocaust: Strategies of Adaptation," *Canadian Journal of Psychiatry* 38 (1993): 384–389; D. B. Whiteman, "Holocaust Survivors and Escapees— Their Strengths," *Psychotherapy* 30 (1993): 443–451.

23   "We create heaven or hell": For persuasive arguments that individuals and not events in and of themselves create stress, see R. S. Lazarus, *Emotion and Adaptation* (New York: Oxford University Press, 1991); R. S. Lazarus and S. Folkman, *Stress, Appraisal, and Coping* (New York: Springer, 1984).

23   "famous story in Zen Buddhism": This story and other similar stories can be found in R. Martin (ed.) and J. Morimoto (illus.), *One Hand Clapping: Zen Stories for All Ages* (New York: Rizzoli International Publishers, 1995).

24   "Wheel of Life": For an in-depth psychological depiction of the Wheel of Life, see M. Epstein, *Thoughts without a Thinker: Psychotherapy from a Buddhist Perspective* (New York: Basic Books, 1995), pp. 15–41.

25   "descent into the underground": The symbolic descent and resurrection theme is represented in many myths and stories. For example, see the account of the Greek goddess Persephone, abducted underground by Hades, in J. S. Bolen, *Goddesses in Every Woman: A New Psychology of Women* (New York: Harper & Row, 1984), chap. 10. The Jungian analyst Sylvia Perera uses the metaphor of descent into the underworld as a means of psychological transformation in her book *Descent to the Goddess: A Way of Initiation for Women* (Toronto, Canada: Inner City Books, 1981).

Notes

25 Macy: Joanna Macy's books include *Despair and Personal Power in the Nuclear Age* (Denver: New Social Publishers, 1983); *Dharma and Development: Religion as a Resource in the Sarvodaya Self-Help Movement* (West Hartford, CT: Kumarian Press, 1983); *Mutual Causality in Buddhism and General Systems Theory: The Dharma of Natural Systems* (New York: State University of New York Press, 1991); *World as Lover, World as Self* (Berkeley, CA: Parallax Press, 1991); J. Robbins and J. Macy, *Diet for a New America: How Your Food Choices Affect Your Health, Happiness, and the Future of Life on Earth* (Walpole, NH: Stillpoint Publishers, 1987).

Part Two

27 Jung: Carl Jung in a letter to V. Subrahamanya Iyer, September 16, 1937. C. G. Jung, *Letters, 1906–1950*, vol. 1 (Princeton, NJ: Princeton University Press, 1973), p. 236.

28 Csikszentmihalyi: See M. Csikszentmihalyi, *The Evolving Self: A Psychology for the Third Millennium* (New York: HarperCollins, 1993), p. 32. For similar perspectives regarding the theory on order out of disorder, see G. Bateson, *Steps to an Ecology of Mind* (New York: Ballantine Books, 1972); I. Prigogine and I. Stengers, *Order Out of Chaos: Man's New Dialogue with Nature* (New York: Bantam Books, 1984).

29 "The roaming mind": M. Csikszentmihalyi, *The Evolving Self*, p. 35.

30 "a man was invited": A version of this story can be found in R. Martin (ed.) and J. Morimoto (illus.), *One Hand Clapping: Zen Stories for All Ages* (New York: Rizzoli International Publishers, 1995).

31 "Suffering always involves a fantasy": See T. H. Ogden, *Matrix of the Mind: Object Relations and the Psychoanalytic Dialogue* (Northvale, NJ: Jason Aronson, 1986).

31 Jung: See note for p. 9.

35 Gottlieb: Dan Gottlieb has already authored one book, *Family Matters: Healing in the Heart of the Family* (New York: NAL/Dutton, 1991), and is in the process of writing a second book. He writes

Notes

a bimonthly newspaper column for the *Philadelphia Inquirer* and is the national radio talk-show host of "Voices in the Family" for WHYY in Philadelphia.

42 "Many myths and stories": Well known among these stories are those of Jesus and the Buddha, as well as tales of many other divinities and saints. Sylvia Perera Brinton's *Descent to the Goddess* (see note for p. 25) is an account of the goddess Inanna's willing journey to the underworld.

51 "psychological complexes": For a review of Jung's theory of psychological complexes, see C. G. Jung, "A Review of the Complex Theory" in vol. 8 of *The Collected Works of C. G. Jung*, 2d ed., trans. R. F. C. Hull (Princeton, NJ: Princeton University Press, 1959), pp. 92–104. Also see Jung in *The Collected Works*, 2d ed., vol. 2, pp. 598–603.

Jung's later theory of complexes included the idea that every complex is characterized by an emotional state that emanates from a core archetypal image. The complex itself is a collection of associated bits of experience (e.g., idea, habits, sensations) that cohere through a common emotional state or meaning. An archetype is a universal tendency to form a particular coherent image (e.g., the Great Mother) in a particular emotional state (e.g., satisfaction). A complex becomes a subpersonality of the unconscious when it is enacted or experienced repeatedly. (See note for p. 54, "structures of personality.")

52 "Great Mother": The Great Mother represents the fullness of nurture, the fantasized sense of completeness or merger. The image of Great Mother is depicted in all world mythologies, often in reference to both human mothers and nature. One Greek image of the Great Mother is Aphrodite, the mother of Eros—seductive, gratifying, and extremely adoring. Another is Demeter, mother of Persephone—devoted, nurturant, powerful, and persuasive.

52 "Terrible Mother": The Terrible Mother represents felt rejection and abandonment. The expression of this archetype is to be found in tales of witches, mean stepmothers, and old hags. One

Notes

Greek version of the Terrible Mother is Jocasta, who abandons her infant son Oedipus and then uses him later for her own sexual pleasure.

53 "projection": For Jung's definition of projection, see his *Collected Works*, vol. 6, p. 457. Also see G. E. Vaillant, *Adaptation to Life* (Boston: Little, Brown, 1977).

54 "structures of personality": Psychological complexes are necessary forms of organization in the human personality. They are ways of encoding memories and directing our behavior so that we adapt to our early circumstances. Often the term *complex* has a negative connotation in our culture and we may feel ashamed when we are "caught" in a complex. I want to stress that one is not to blame for one's complexes and that, without them, we would not have survived our early lives. Whether complexes are positive or negative, they are adaptive to our early lives, but are often unadaptive later.

Complexes are emotionally charged because their image-traces go back to our earliest relationships when we were helpless and powerless. Complexes often operate outside of our conscious awareness and strongly influence our behavior. When activated, individuals sometimes feel possessed or strongly compelled to act on their "gut feelings." Jung described the power of complexes when he wrote, "The psychic energy applies itself wholly to the complex at the expense of other psychic material, which in consequence remains unused. All stimuli that do not suit the complex undergo a partial apperceptive degeneration with emotional impoverishment. . . . On the other hand the slightest remark even remotely touching on the complex instantly arouses a violent outburst of anger or pain." *The Collected Works*, vol. 3, p. 48.

54 "archetype": See C. G. Jung, *The Collected Works*, vol. 9.1. For a full treatment of the evolution of the term *archetype* in Jung's work, see P. Young-Eisendrath and J. Hall, *Jung's Self Psychology: A Constructivist Perspective* (New York: Guilford Press, 1991). My definition of *archetype* fits primarily with Jung's work on the

concept after 1944. He changes what was initially an essentialist (Kantian) concept of "mental image" to something akin to
an "innate releasing mechanism" in evolutionary biology. Jung's
later definition refers to a predisposition to form a coherent
image in emotionally aroused states. For example, human beings are "prewired" to form images of Great and Terrible Mothers universally, no matter the culture. Archetypes are familiar
the world over because they derive from common human emotions. Archetypal images cohere at first in states of powerful
affect during our powerless infancy. They continue to arouse us
later in predictable ways. When we are living out an archetype,
rather than sensing it as emanating from our own attitudes and
perceptions, we are captured by primitive states (from idealized
love to terror) that can be extremely distressing.

55 "karma": For a discussion of karma by Jung, see his *Collected
Works*, vol. 11.

55 Dharmasiri: See G. Dharmasiri, *Buddhist Ethics* (Antioch, CA:
Golden Leaves Publishing, 1989).

56 "stretch back over the generations": There is empirical evidence
from researchers in the field of infant-mother attachment sup-
porting the intergenerational transmission of relational patterns.
I. Bretherton, "Attachment Theory: Retrospect and Prospect,"
in I. Bretherton and E. Waters (eds.), *Growing Points of Attachment
Theory and Research. Monographs of the Society for Research in Child
Development* 501 (1985): 3–37; I. Bretherton, "Communication
Patterns, Internal Working Models, and the Intergenerational
Transmission of Attachment Relationships," *Infant Mental Health
Journal* 11, no. 3 (1990): 237–252; K. Grossmann et al., "Ma-
ternal Attachment Representations as Related to Patterns of
Infant-Mother Attachment and Maternal Care during the First
Year," in R. A. Hinde and J. Stevenson-Hinde (eds.), *Relationships
within Families* (Oxford: Oxford University Press, 1988);
M. Ricks, "The Social Transmission of Parental Behavior: At-
tachment across Generations," in I. Bretherton and E. Waters
(eds.), *Growing Points of Attachment Theory and Research. Monographs*

of the Society for Research in Child Development 501 (1985): 211–230;
M. H. Van Ijzendoorn, "Intergenerational Transmission of Parenting: A Review of Studies in Nonclinical Populations," *Developmental Review* 12 (1992): 76–99.

57   Jung: See note for p. 55 on Jung's theory of karma.

57   "A karma always attains": Dharmasiri, *Buddhist Ethics*, p. 37.

58   Wilber: K. Wilber and T. K. Wilber, *Grace and Grit: Spirituality and Healing in the Life and Death of Treya Killan Wilber* (Boston: Shambhala, 1994), p. 283.

Page   *Part Three*

61   "I Ching": See C. F. Baynes and R. Wilhelm (trans.), *The I Ching: The Richard Wilhelm Translation*, 3d ed. (Princeton, NJ: Princeton University Press, 1967), p. 16.

62   "popular psychology": The popularity of using affirmations as a means of overcoming the wounded self-image that results from a difficult childhood is reflected in the explosion of books filled with "daily affirmations" of the self. Such books are readily found in the "codependent" and "recovery" sections of many bookstores.

63   "not simply survivors": In the words of resiliency researchers Werner and Smith, the resilient person "works well, loves well, and expects well." See E. E. Werner and R. S. Smith, *Vulnerable but Invincible: A Study of Resilient Children* (New York: McGraw-Hill, 1982). Also see G. O. Higgins, *Resilient Adults: Overcoming a Cruel Past* (San Francisco: Jossey-Bass, 1994); C. Kaufmann et al., "Superkids: Competent Children of Psychotic Mothers," *American Journal of Psychiatry* 136 (1979): 1398–1402; E. E. Werner, "High-Risk Children in Young Adulthood: A Longitudinal Study from Birth to 32 Years," *American Journal of Orthopsychiatry* 59, no. 1 (1989): 72–81; D. B. Whiteman, "Holocaust Survivors and Escapees—Their Strengths," *Psychotherapy* 30 (1993): 443–451.

63   "thought it folly to believe": See note for p. 19 on "secure attachments."

Notes

64   "one in ten": See E. J. Anthony, "The Syndrome of the Psychologically Invulnerable Child," in A. E. Koupernil (ed.), *The Child in His Family: Children at Psychiatric Risk* (New York: Wiley, 1974), pp. 529–544; C. Kaufmann et al., "Superkids;" M. Rutter, "Early Sources of Security and Competence," in J. Bruner and J. Garten (eds.), *Human Growth and Development* (New York: Oxford University Press, 1978).

    A widely cited and well-known study is that of seven hundred children from the island of Kauai, Hawaii, who were followed from birth to thirty-two years of age. From these children we know that one in ten people who grew up in difficult conditions—with the strain of poverty, family conflicts, and other adversities that placed them at risk for later chaos in their lives—is exceptionally competent as an adult. By competent, I mean doing something worthwhile *and* feeling grateful, successful, and self-confident. For a summary of the research findings, see Werner, "High-Risk Children in Young Adulthood."

64   "invulnerable or invincible": These terms were traditionally used to describe children who, contrary to expectation, did not develop psychological disorders from childhood emotional or physical abuse. Today, researchers conceive of the resilient or stress-resistant as individuals who cope successfully with adverse circumstances or have a greater likelihood of successful adaptation despite their high-risk status. See E. J. Anthony and B. J. Cohler (eds.), *The Invulnerable Child* (New York: Guilford Press, 1987); N. Garmezy, "Vulnerability Research and the Issue of Primary Prevention," *American Journal of Orthopsychiatry* 41 (1971): 101–116; A. S. Masten and N. Garmezy, "Risk, Vulnerability, and Protective Factors in Developmental Psychopathology," in B. B. Lahey and A. E. Kazdin (eds.), *Advances in Clinical Child Psychology*, vol. 8 (New York: Plenum, 1985), pp. 1–52; M. Rutter, "Psychosocial Resilience and Protective Mechanisms," in J. Rolf, A. S. Masten, D. Cicchetti, K. H. Nuechterlein, and S. Weintraub (eds.), *Risk and Protective Factors in the Development of Psychopathology* (Cambridge, England: Cambridge

University Press, 1990), pp. 181–214; E. E. Werner and R. S. Smith, *Vulnerable but Invincible.* (New York: McGraw-Hill, 1982).

64 "many lead effective lives": S. Hauser et al., "Vulnerability and Resilience in Adolescence: Views from the Family," *Journal of Adolescence 5*, no. 1 (1985): 81–100. Manfred Bleuler, in his longitudinal study, found that 75 percent of children who had parents with mental illness were psychologically competent as adults. See M. Bleuler, *The Schizophrenic Disorders: Long-term Patient and Family Studies* (New Haven: Yale University Press, 1978). In addition, reviews of the research on victims of childhood physical abuse generally agree that two-thirds of those who are abused in childhood do *not* go on to be child abusers in adulthood. See, for example, J. Kaufman and E. Zigler, "Do Abused Children Become Abusive Parents?" *American Journal of Orthopsychiatry 57*, no. 2 (1987): 186–192.

64 "may not be a life": A. S. Masten and N. Garmezy, "Risk, Vulnerability, and Protective Factors," p. 13.

68 "more than constitutional factors": Although not denying the role of constitutional factors, the protective role of factors other than constitution has been supported by numerous studies. To review research and quote, see M. Rutter, "Psychosocial Resilience and Protective Mechanisms," p. 183.

It is noteworthy that although an easy temperament has traditionally been found to operate as a protective factor against stress, this may not always be the case. A study conducted by de Vries found that infants with a difficult temperament were significantly more likely to survive in the midst of a severe drought than children with easy temperaments. See M. W. de Vries, "Temperament and Infant Mortality among the Masai of East Africa," *American Journal of Psychiatry 141* (1984): 1189–1194.

68 "six major childhood stressors": Researcher Michael Rutter derived these six factors from his longitudinal study of children on the Isle of Wight in England. He found that the effect of the number of stressors is not simply additive but multiplicative:

The presence of two risk factors was associated with a fourfold increase in risk as compared with the presence of zero or one factor, while four or more risk factors was related to a tenfold increase in susceptibility to risk. See M. Rutter, "Protective Factors in Children's Responses to Stress and Disadvantage," in M. W. Kent and J. Rolf (eds.), *Primary Prevention of Psychopathology*, vol. 3 (Hanover, NH: University Press of New England, 1979), pp. 49–74; Rutter, "Psychosocial Resilience;" M. Rutter et al., *Fifteen Thousand Hours: Secondary Schools and Their Effects on Children* (Cambridge, England: Cambridge University Press, 1979); Rutter et al., "Attainment and Adjustment in Two Geographical Areas: III. Some Factors Accounting for Area Differences," *British Journal of Psychiatry* 126 (1975): 520–533.

69　"resilient react to childhood stresses": Across a number of empirical studies, resilient youth were significantly more likely to respond to stress with optimism, an internal locus of control, and a sense of self-efficacy as compared with the children who were not resilient. See E. L. Cowen et al., "The Rochester Child Resilience Project: Overview and Summary of First Year Findings," *Development and Psychopathology* 2 (1990): 193–212; S. B. Fine, "Resilience and Human Adaptability: Who Rises above Adversity?" *American Journal of Occupational Therapy* 45, no. 6 (1991): 493–502; Kaufman and Zigler, "Do Abused Children Become Abusive Parents?"; D. O'Grady and J. R. Metz, "Resilience in Children at High Risk for Psychiatric Disorder," *Journal of Pediatric Psychology* 12 (1987): 3–23.

69　"vulnerable": Ann Masten and Norman Garmezy point out that the susceptibility to a negative outcome in the face of stress is not solely a result of either genetic or environmental factors but rather both factors as they interact in a nonadditive fashion. See Masten and Garmezy, *Advances in Clinical Child Psychology*.

69　"statistics on sexual and physical abuse": In a national survey of adults, 27 percent of the women and 16 percent of the men reported experiencing some form of sexual abuse in childhood. See D. Finkelhor et al., "Sexual Abuse in a National Survey of

Adult Men and Women: Prevalence, Characteristics, and Risk Factors," *Child Abuse and Neglect* 14 (1990): 19–28. A government report suggested that 62 percent of girls and 31 percent of boys were suspected to have experienced childhood sexual abuse. See H. Dubowitz, "Child Maltreatment in the United States: Etiology, Impact, and Prevention," a paper prepared for the Congress of the United States (Washington, DC: Office of Technology Assessment, 1986). In addition, Diana Russell reported in *The Secret Trauma: Incest in the Lives of Girls and Women* (New York: Basic Books, 1987) that more than 38 percent of the 933 women she surveyed reported being victims of sexual abuse prior to age eighteen.

The difficulty of determining accurate estimates of sexual abuse is based in part on the various research methods and survey questions. After an extensive review of the existing empirical studies, David Finkelhor in "The Sexual Abuse of Children: Current Research Reviewed," *Psychiatric Annals: The Journal of Continuing Psychiatric Education* 17, no. 4 (1987): 233–241, suggested that at least 5 percent of adults report some type of sexual abuse in childhood, with survey results ranging between 6 to 62 percent for women and 3 to 31 percent for men.

The statistics on the rates of physical abuse are just as troubling. Four in one thousand children are physically abused each year in the United States. See "Study Findings: National Study of the Incidence and Severity of Child Abuse and Neglect," (Washington, DC: U.S. Government Printing Office, 1986). Also see A. H. Cohn, *An Approach to Preventing Child Abuse* (Chicago: National Committee for the Prevention of Child Abuse, 1983); M. A. Straus and R. J. Gelles, "Change in Family Violence from 1975 to 1985," *Journal of Marriage and the Family* 48 (1986): 465–479.

In a national probability sample of 6,002 households, it was reported that 619 out of 1,000 children experienced minor violence and 110 out of 1,000 children experienced severe violence (one out of ten). See G. D. Wolfner and R. J. Gelles,

"A Profile of Violence Toward Children: A National Study,"
Child Abuse and Neglect 17 (1993): 197–212. In another report,
the federal government's National Center on Child Abuse and
Neglect reported that the number of child abuse reports was
2,567,555 nationwide in 1991. See *National Child Abuse and Ne-*
glect Data System: Working Paper 2: 1991 Summary Data Component
(Washington, DC: U.S. Department of Health and Human
Services, 1993).

70 "divorce rate": The rate of marriages was 9.7 per every 1,000
persons in the United States in 1988, while the rate of divorces
and annulments was 4.7 per 1,000. See U.S. National Center
for Health Statistics, *Vital Statistics of the United States* (Washington, DC: National Center for Health Statistics, 1991). Estimations of these same rates based on monthly reports were 9.3 for
marriages and 4.8 for divorces and annulments in 1992. See
U.S. National Center for Health Statistics, *Monthly Vital Statistics*
of the United States (Washington DC: National Center for Health
Statistics, 1993).

70 "Two large surveys of college students": Segal and Figley found
that 80 percent of male and female college students experienced
one or more highly stressful events by the age of eighteen years.
See S. Segal and C. Figley, "Stressful Events," *Hospital and Com-*
munity Psychiatry 39, no. 9 (1988): 998; D. Lauterbach and
S. Vrana, "Incidence of Traumatic Events and Post-Traumatic
Psychological Symptoms among College Students" (paper presented at the 63d annual meeting of the Midwestern Psychological Association, Chicago, May 1991).

70 "characteristic of the resilient": The predictors of resilience
compiled by Cox in *Childhood Adversity* were based on the psychoanalytic theory of Heinz Kohut; see H. Kohut, *The Restora-*
tion of the Self (New York: International Universities Press, 1977);
H. Kohut, *How Does Analysis Cure* (Chicago: University of Chicago Press, 1984). Our review of the research consistently
suggests that the following traits characterize the resilient:
higher IQ, better self-esteem, self-worth, and self-regard (rather

than self-derogation), eagerness to learn and active goal-directed behavior, greater perceived competence, better social skills, more social responsivity, more optimistic views, a sense of power (rather than powerlessness), an internal locus of control and realistic control attributions, empathy, creativity, and humor. See Cowen et al., "The Rochester Child Resilience Project;" Fine, "Resilience and Human Adaptability"; N. Garmezy, "Resiliency and Vulnerability to Adverse Developmental Outcomes Associated with Poverty," *American Behavioral Scientist* 34, no. 4 (1991): 416–430; A. S. Masten, P. Morison, D. Pellegrini, and A. Tellegen, "Competence under Stress: Risk and Protective Factors," in J. Rolf, A. S. Masten, D. Cicchetti, K. H. Nuechterlein, and S. Weintraub (eds.), *Risk and Protective Factors in the Development of Psychopathology* (Cambridge, England: Cambridge University Press, 1990), pp. 236–256; D. O'Grady and J. B. Metz, "Resilience in Children."

72 "resilient learn early how to help": The researchers M. Radke-Yarrow and I. Sherman, like previous researchers, noted that the resilients' helpfulness contributed to their development. See M. Bleuler, *The Schizophrenic Disorders*; M. Radke-Yarrow and T. Sherman, "Hard Growing: Children Who Survive," in J. Rolf, A. S. Masten, D. Cicchetti, K. H. Nuechterlein, and S. Weintraub (eds.), *Risk and Protective Factors in the Development of Psychopathology* (Cambridge, England: Cambridge University Press, 1990), pp. 97–119.

73 Macy: See note for p. 25.

74 "we're attracted to particular people": The research on intergenerational transmission of relational patterns lends credence to the hypothesis that we are drawn to people who are like our parents. For excellent discussions on why this intergenerational transmission occurs, see J. Bowlby, *A Secure Base: Parent-Child Attachment and Healthy Human Development* (New York: Basic Books, 1988); L. A. Sroufe and J. Fleeson, "Attachment and the Construction of Relationships," in W. Hartup and Z. Rubin (eds.), *Relationships and Development* (Hillsdale, NJ: Lawrence Erlbaum,

1986), pp. 51–71. Sroufe, like John Bowlby, suggests that we internalize both sides of our childhood relationships. He depicts how we're selectively attracted to people who complement our childhood relational roles, which in turn perpetuates these patterns.

74 Higgins: Gina Higgins's in-depth interviews of resilient adults are described in her book *Resilient Adults*.

75 Shibvon: Ibid., p. 33.

76 Shibvon: Ibid., p. 34.

76 "children who were reared by emotionally ill parents": These resilient adolescents were at extremely high risk for future maladjustment based on their genetic (one or both parents had a psychiatric disorder) and environmental backgrounds. All 25 of them were selected from a study of 123 families, approximately half of whom had one or two parents with a history of a depressive disorder and half with no history of psychiatric illness. See M. Radke-Yarrow and T. Sherman, "Hard Growing: Children Who Survive."

77 Bleuler: See Bleuler, *The Schizophrenic Disorders*. For a condensed summary of Bleuler's findings, see N. Garmezy, "Stress-Resistant Children: The Search for Protective Factors," in J. E. Stevenson (ed.), *Recent Research in Developmental Psychopathology* (New York: Pergamon Press, 1985), pp. 213–233.

78 Cox: See A. L. Cox, "Childhood Adversity and the Successful, Resilient Black Adult: A Retrospective Qualitative Study" (Ph.D. diss., Smith College School for Social Work, 1994).

79 "how little help most had": The resilient interviewed for both Higgins's and Cox's qualitative studies report that there was no adult in their childhood who helped them cope with their situation or provided solace from it on a regular basis. I, too, have often informally noted this in my clinical experience. See A. L. Cox, *Childhood Adversity*; and G. O. Higgins, *Resilient Adults*, pp. 324–325. Emmy Werner, in her study of the children of Kauai, reported that the resilient children were successful in selecting positive role models in the community (e.g., teachers,

clergy). Other researchers have noted how the resilient find solace in school and reading: Michael Rutter reported that the resilient subjects in his study had more positive school experiences than the nonresilient subjects and that this played a protective role later in life; M. Rutter and D. Quinton, "Long-term Follow up of Women Institutionalized in Childhood: Factors Promoting Good Functioning in Adult Life," *British Journal of Developmental Psychology* 2 (1984): 191–204; E. E. Werner, "High-Risk Children."

81 "feeling different from one's family": No one has yet scientifically investigated this relationship, so it is empirically unsubstantiated. However, the individuals interviewed for this book reported that they felt different from others in their childhoods, and similar findings are reported in G. O. Higgins, *Resilient Adults.*

83 "survivors of the Holocaust": See R. Krell, "Child Survivors of the Holocaust: Strategies of Adaptation," *Canadian Journal of Psychiatry* 38 (1993): 384–389; D. B. Whiteman, "Holocaust Survivors."

83 "optimism": See M. F. Scheier, J. K. Weintraub, and C. S. Carver, "Coping with Stress: Divergent Strategies of Optimists and Pessimists," *Journal of Personality and Social Psychology* 51, no. 6 (1986): 1257–1264.

The results from the study "The Rochester Child Resilience Project," by E. L. Cowen et al., suggest that stress-resistant children are indeed more optimistic. There is a substantial body of empirical literature in the field of social psychology on coping, stress, and psychological adjustment among adults. A few examples of this research literature include C. S. Carver and J. G. Gaines, "Optimism, Pessimism, and Postpartum Depression," *Cognitive Therapy and Research* 11, no. 4 (1987): 449–462; M. F. Scheier and C. S. Carver, "Dispositional Optimism and Physical Well-being: The Influence of Generalized Outcome Expectancies on Health," *Journal of Personality* 52, no. 2 (1987): 169–210; C. J. Holahan and R. H. Moos, "Personality,

Notes

Coping, and Family Resources in Stress Resistance," *Journal of Personality and Social Psychology* 51 (1986): 389–395; R. S. Lazarus and S. Folkman, *Stress, Appraisal, and Coping* (New York: Springer, 1984); R. S. Lazarus, A. D. Kanner, and S. Folkman, "Emotions: A Cognitive-Phenomenological Analysis," in R. Pluttchik and H. Kellerman (eds.), *Emotion: Theory, Research, and Experience* (New York: Academic Press, 1980), pp. 189–217.

84 Shibvon: G. O. Higgins, *Resilient Adults*, p. 40.

86 Muller: W. Muller, *Legacy of the Heart: The Spiritual Advantages of a Painful Childhood* (New York: S & S Trade, 1993).

87 "spiritual context": See G. O. Higgins, *Resilient Adults*, for a description of the spirituality of her subjects. Most of the evidence of the role of spirituality of the resilient is anecdotal, although there is some scientific basis for this claim. Studies suggest that the resilient tend to be church members or to possess a deep sense of spirituality. See S. B. Fine, "Resilience and Human Adaptability"; R. E. Gray, "Adolescent Response to the Death of a Parent," *Journal of Youth and Adolescence* 16 (1987): 511–525; L. Valentine and L. L. Feinauer, "Resilience Factors Associated with Female Survivors of Childhood Sexual Abuse," *American Journal of Family Therapy* 21 (1993): 216–224.

87 "sense of coherence": Aaron Antonovsky suggested that the field of stress research would benefit by enlarging its empirical focus on life stress and subsequent psychopathology to include "salutogenesis" or the study of health promotion. Similar to resiliency researchers, he shifted the emphasis from failures in coping to characteristics associated with health and success. His three themes associated with health come from a qualitative study of individuals who were coping successfully or unsuccessfully with a very large number of life stressors. He found that a sense of coherence distinguished successful from unsuccessful copers. These three dimensions of coherence support my claim that meaning, purpose, and hope are critical to successfully coping with adversity. See A. Antonovsky, *Unraveling the Mystery*

of Health: How People Manage Stress and Stay Well (San Francisco: Jossey-Bass, 1987).

88 "emperor": A rendition of this story can be found in R. Martin (ed.) and J. Morimoto (illus.), *One Hand Clapping: Zen Stories for All Ages* (New York: Rizzoli International Publishers, 1995).

91 Jung: See C. G. Jung, *The Collected Works of C. G. Jung*, 2d ed., vol. 11., trans. R. F. C. Hull (Princeton, NJ: Princeton University Press, 1959); also see Jung in F. M. Bockus, "The Archetypal Self: Theological Values in Jung's Psychology," in R. L. Moore and D. J. Meckel (eds.), *Jung and Christianity in Dialogue: Faith, Feminism, and Hermeneutics* (Mahwah, NY: Paulist Press, 1990); D. J. Meckel and R. L. Moore (eds.), *Self and Liberation: The Jung-Buddhism Dialogue* (Mahwah, NY: Paulist Press, 1992). Proposing that spirituality promotes psychological wholeness, Jung wrote, "Religious ideas and convictions from the beginning of history had the aspect of mental *pharmakon*. They represent the world of *wholeness* in which fragments can be gathered and put together again. Such a cure cannot be effected by pills and injections." C. G. Jung, 1953, *Letters, 1951–1961*, vol. 2 (Princeton, NJ: Princeton University Press, 1975), p. 625.

92 "conscious attitude": Jung offers this idea in many places throughout his work. For example, at a Congress of the Society of Public Health in Zurich, in 1929, Jung said, "The task of psychotherapy is to correct the conscious attitude and not to go chasing after the infantile memories. Naturally you cannot do the one without paying attention to the other, but the main emphasis should be upon the attitude of the patient. There are extremely practical reasons for this, because there is scarcely a neurotic who does not love to dwell upon the evils of the past and to wallow in self-commiserating memories. Very often his neurosis consists precisely in his hanging back and constantly excusing himself on account of the past." C. G. Jung, *The Collected Works*, 2d ed., vol. 16, pp. 31–32.

93 "religious beliefs": See note for p. 87.

Notes

94 "girls tend to underestimate": A number of studies have found that girls, despite their equivalent achievement scores and grades, provide lower estimations of their performance and competence and assume that their successes are due to hard work or luck instead of their ability. Boys overestimate their performance and believe their successes are due to their ability and intelligence. This finding held true even for early adolescent males and females who scored at or above the 98th percentile on a math aptitude test. See V. J. Crandall, "Sex Differences in Expectancy of Intellectual and Academic Performance," in R. Unger and F. Denmark (eds.), *Women: Dependent or Independent Variable?* (New York: Psychological Dimensions, 1975), pp. 649–685; C. Dweck et al., "Sex Differences in Learned Helplessness: II. The Contingencies of Evaluative Feedback in the Classroom and III. An Experimental Analysis," *Developmental Psychology* 14 (1978): 268–276; E. Fennema and G. Leder (eds.), *Mathematics and Gender* (New York: Teachers College Press, Columbia University, 1990); L. Kramer, "Gifted Adolescent Girls: Self-perceptions of Ability within One Middle School Setting" (Ph.D. diss., University of Florida, 1985); D. J. Stipek, "Sex Differences in Children's Attributions for Success and Failure on Math and Spelling Tests," *Sex Roles* 11 (1984): 969–981. For an excellent discussion of the origins and consequences of this gender difference in ability estimations in the popular press, see J. Mann, *The Difference: Growing Up Female in America* (New York: Warner Books, 1994).

94 "receive different treatment in the classroom": The different treatment boys and girls receive in the classroom leads to assertiveness in boys and passivity in girls. Boys receive more criticism, are asked more challenging questions, and are given more instruction. See M. Sadker and D. Sadker, *Failing at Fairness: How America's Schools Cheat Girls* (New York: Macmillan, 1994).

95 "relinquish their ambitions": The empirical literature suggests that adolescent females sacrifice their academic achievement for

the sake of popularity. Girls learn to sacrifice achievement and assertiveness—long-term successes—for a short-term gratification—popularity; see "The Gangly Years," *Psychology Today,* September 1987, pp. 28–34. See also G. R. Adams and J. L. Roopnarine, "Physical Attractiveness, Social Skills, and Same-Sex Peer Popularity," *Journal of Group Psychotherapy-Psychodrama-and-Sociometry* 47 (1994): 15–35; J. Coleman, *The Adolescent Society* (New York: Free Press, 1961).

95 "girls' losses of self-confidence and achievement and voice": A substantial number of studies have demonstrated that girls' self-esteem and confidence decline significantly across the middle school years as compared with those of boys. See B. Allgood-Merten, P. Lewinsohn, and H. Hops, "Sex Differences and Adolescent Depression," *Journal of Abnormal Psychology* 91, no. 1 (1990): 55–63; American Association of University Women, *Shortchanging Girls, Shortchanging America* (Washington, D.C.: Greenberg-Lake, 1991); B. Herman, "Changing Sources of Self-Esteem among Boys and Girls in Secondary Schools," *Urban Education* 24 (1990): 432–439; B. E. Kline and E. B. Short, "Changes in Emotional Resilience: Gifted Adolescent Females," *Roeper Review* 13, no. 3 (1991): 118–121; P. B. Moran and J. Eckenrode, "Gender Differences in the Costs and Benefits of Peer Relationships during Adolescence," *Journal of Adolescent Research* 6, no. 4 (1991): 396–409; L. M. Brown and C. Gilligan, *Meeting at the Crossroads: Women's Psychology and Girl's Development* (Cambridge, MA: Harvard University Press, 1992).

95 "score higher on measures of distress": Results of empirical studies consistently suggest that women experience significantly more depression than men. See W. W. Eaton and L. G. Kessler, *Epidemiologic Field Methods in Psychiatry: The NIMH Epidemiologic Catchment Area Program* (Orlando, FL: Academic Press, 1985); Kline and Short, "Changes in Emotional Resilience"; P. M. Lewinsohn et al., "Adolescent Psychopathology: II. Psychosocial Risk Factors for Depression," *Journal of Abnormal Psychology* 103, no. 2 (1994): 302–315; S. Nolen-Hoeksema,

"Sex Differences in Unipolar Depression: Evidence and Theory," *Psychological Bulletin* 101, no. 2 (1987): 259–282; M. M. Weissman and G. L. Klerman, "Sex Differences and the Epidemiology of Depression," *Archives of General Psychiatry* 34 (1977): 98–111.

95 "sexual abuse": Numerous reviews of the empirical literature on childhood sexual abuse suggest that women are significantly more likely to have been sexually abused during childhood than men. See D. Finkelhor, "Epidemiological Factors in the Clinical Identification of Child Sexual Abuse," *Child Abuse and Neglect* 17 (1993): 67–70; D. Finkelhor and J. Dzluba-Leatherman, *The Victimization of Children*; D. Finkelhor et al., "Sexual Abuse in a National Survey of Adult Men and Women: Prevalence, Characteristics, and Risk Factors," *Child Abuse and Neglect* 14 (1990): 19–28; M. Wellman, "Child Sexual Abuse and Gender Differences: Attitudes and Prevalence," *Child Abuse and Neglect* 17, no. 4 (1993): 539–547.

96 "girls are generally more resilient": Research suggests that, as long as the primary caretaker is available, female children are more resilient than males. See M. Rutter, "Sex Differences in Children's Responses to Family Stress," in E. J. Anthony and C. Koupernick (eds.), *The Child in His Family*, vol. 1 (New York: Wiley, 1970); M. Rutter, "Epidemiological-Longitudinal Approaches to the Study of Development," in W. A. Collins (ed.), *The Concept of Development, Minnesota Symposia on Child Psychology*, vol. 15, (Hillsdale, NJ: Lawrence Erlbaum, 1982); E. E. Werner and R. S. Smith, *Vulnerable but Invincible*.

Some empirical evidence suggests that females may become more vulnerable at adolescence, despite their previous advantage over males. See A. S. Masten, "Toward a Developmental Psychopathology of Early Adolescence," in M. D. Levine and E. R. McAnarney (eds.), *Early Adolescent Transitions* (Lexington, MA: D. C. Heath, 1988), pp. 261–278; E. E. Werner and R. S. Smith, *Vulnerable but Invincible*.

96 "Boys show more symptoms of aggression. . . . Girls show more

anxiety and depression": It is typically the case that boys respond to stress with more externalizing behaviors (i.e., outwardly directed behavior, e.g., aggression, hyperactivity, and drug abuse) and girls with more of a tendency to internalizing (e.g., depression, anxiety). As part of a longitudinal study of nonclinical adolescents, Per Gjerde and Jack and Jeanne Block found that eighteen-year-old males with depression were rated as disagreeable, aggressive, and antagonistic (i.e., labeled an externalizing pattern), while depressed females were characterized as ego-brittle, unconventional, and ruminating (i.e., an internalizing pattern). See P. F. Gjerde, J. Block, and J. H. Block, "Depressive Symptoms and Personality during Late Adolescence: Gender Differences in the Externalization-Internalization of Symptom Expression," *Journal of Abnormal Psychology* 97, no. 4 (1988): 475–486. In another study of 180 six- to twelve-year-olds, girls had significantly more internalizing disorders than boys. See N. J. Cohen, "Sex Differences in Child Psychiatric Outpatients: Cognitive, Personality, and Behavioral Characteristics," *Child Psychiatry and Human Development* 20, no. 2 (1989): 113–121. Also see D. B. Levit, "Gender Differences in Ego Defenses in Adolescence: Sex Role as One Way to Understand the Differences," *Journal of Personality and Social Psychology* 61, no. 6 (1991): 992–999.

96 "unreachable expectations": It has been pointed out how the typical encouragement of boys to pursue unrealistically high career aspirations, when not obtained, leads to chronic feelings of failure. See M. Komarovsky, *Dilemmas of Masculinity: A Study of College Youth* (New York: W. W. Norton, 1976); J. Pleck and R. Brannon, "Male Roles and the Male Experience," *Journal of Social Issues* 34 (1978): 1–4.

Although males are privy to certain advantages, it is questionable whether this socialization is constructive in the long run. A number of statistics demonstrate that older males are exposed to and are victims of various forms of violence at a rate alarmingly higher than that of females. Consider the following sample of statistics: Boys are three times more likely to become alcohol dependent and 50 percent more likely to use illicit drugs than females. Men account for more than 90 percent of alcohol- and drug-related arrests. See W. D. Watts and L. S. Wright, "The Relationship of Alcohol, Tobacco, Marijuana, and Other Illegal Drug Use to Delinquency among Mexican-American, Black, and White Adolescent Males," *Adolescence* 25 (1990): 171–181. Males' recklessness is also apparent in auto accident rates. The leading cause of death among fifteen- to twenty-four-year-old white males is accidents. See Children's Defense Fund, *The State of America's Children: 1992* (Washington, DC: Children's Defense Fund, 1992).

97 "buffered by stable caregivers": In reviewing the empirical literature, Norman Garmezy identified three common factors associated with resilience: (1) personality dispositions such as an easy temperament, self-esteem, and internal locus of control; (2) the presence of a warm supportive family atmosphere; and (3) the presence of an external support system that reinforces the child's efforts to cope with adversity. See "Stress-Resistant Children: The Search for Protective Factors," in J. E. Stevenson (ed.), *Recent Research in Developmental Psychopathology* (New York: Pergamon Press, 1985), pp. 213–233.

Conversely, low self-esteem, a lack of self-determination, hopelessness, and helplessness tend to place children at risk. See, for example, A. L. Baldwin, C. Baldwin, and R. E. Cole, "Stress-Resistant Families and Stress-Resistant Children," in J. Rolf, A. S. Masten, D. Cicchetti, K. H. Nuechterlein, and S. Weintraub (eds.), *Risk and Protective Factors in the Development of Psychopathology* (Cambridge, England: Cambridge University Press, 1990), pp. 257–280; E. L. Cowen et al., "The Rochester Child Resilience Project;" L. Fisher et al., "Competent Children at Risk: A Study of Well-Functioning Offspring of Disturbed Parents," in E. J. Anthony and B. J. Cohler (eds.), *The Invulnerable Child* (New York: Guilford Press, 1987), pp. 211–228; M. Rutter, "Early Sources of Security."

97 "Overt and covert messages": I have discussed our culture's social context that condones appearance as a source of power for women. See P. Young-Eisendrath and F. Wiedemann, *Female Authority: Empowering Women through Psychotherapy* (New York: Guilford Press, 1987), pp. 19–22.

97 "feedback that your efforts are working": It appears that gradual successes with increasing levels of adversity or difficulty are a critical ingredient of resilience. Graduated successes also referred to as "inoculation" are more likely if the strategies necessary to overcome the adversity are within the individual's developmental level or competence. See N. Garmezy, "Stress-Resistant Children"; J. A. Schaefer and R. H. Moos, "Life Crises and Personal Growth," in B. N. Carpenter (ed.), *Personal Coping: Theory, Research, and Applications* (Westport, CT: Praeger, 1992), pp. 149–170. Similarly, Michael Rutter has used the metaphor of immunization to convey the benefits of graduated successes in dealing with stress. See M. Rutter, "Psychosocial Resilience." According to Martin Seligman's theory of learned helplessness, a sense of self-efficacy is critical to psychological health. See J. Garber and M. F. P. Seligman (eds.), *Human Helplessness: Theory and Application* (New York: Academic Press, 1980); C. Peterson, S. F. Maier, and M. F. P. Seligman, *Learned Helplessness: A Theory for the Age of Personal Control* (New York: Oxford University Press, 1993); M. F. P. Seligman, *Helplessness: On Depression, Development, and Death* (San Francisco: W. H. Freeman, 1975).

Page   *Part Four*

99 Fowler: G. Fowler, *Dance of a Fallen Monk: The Twists and Turns of a Spiritual Life* (Reading, MA: Addison-Wesley, 1995), p. 276.

99 "True Self": The *true self*, according to D. W. Winnicott, is the individual's inborn potential for a unique personality, the source of authenticity and spontaneity. When there are failures in parenting, the child constructs a secondary or false self. The *false self* is a compliant, defensive persona presented to the outside world in order to protect the inner self from psychic

annihilation. See D. W. Winnicott: "Ego Distortion in Terms of True and False Self," in *The Maturational Process and the Facilitating Environment* (New York: International Universities Press, 1960), pp. 140–152; *Human Nature* (New York: Schocken Books, 1988); *Playing and Reality* (London: Tavistock, 1971).

Many psychotherapists conceive of a true (real or authentic) self and a false self, the latter generally believed to result from intrusive, neglectful, or deeply unempathic parenting. Jung's early definitions of the "archetype of the self" tend to characterize the self as an inborn "supraordinate personality" or preexisting organization that is metaphorized in images of the center, the king, the union of opposites, and so on. Jung's early theory resembles Winnicott's true self. See C. G. Jung, *The Collected Works of C. G. Jung*, 2d ed., vol. 6, trans. R. F. C. Hull (Princeton, NJ: Princeton University Press, 1959), p. 460. In his later work Jung talks about the self as an "empty center" or the underlying *principle* of organization: "The whole course of individuation is dialectical, and the so-called 'end' is the confrontation of the ego with the 'emptiness' of the centre. Here the limit of possible experience is reached; the ego dissolves as the reference point of cognition." This is quoted from a letter Jung wrote to a Swiss pastor in 1955. It appears in C. G. Jung, *Letters, 1951–1961*, vol. 2 (Princeton, NJ: Princeton University Press, 1975), p. 259. In these later examples, Jung sometimes sounds as though he takes the perspective of no-self. Jung's writings can be used in defense of either the True Self or a no-self understanding of individual subjectivity. I prefer to see Jung as having moved in his later life to a position about the self that is consonant with the no-self of Buddhism.

100 "make a 'self' out of changing subjective states and roles": The psychiatrist Mark Epstein, in his recent book about Buddhism and psychoanalysis, puts it this way: "We define ourselves by our moods and by our thoughts. We do not just let ourselves be happy or sad . . . we must become a happy person or a sad

one." See M. Epstein, *Thoughts without a Thinker: Psychotherapy from a Buddhist Perspective* (New York: Basic Books, 1995), p. 77.

100   "The realization of impermanence": See Sogyal Rinpoche, *The Tibetan Book of Living and Dying* (San Francisco: HarperSanFrancisco, 1992), p. 25.

100   "self is a function": See M. Epstein, *Thoughts without a Thinker;* J. Piaget, *Six Psychological Studies* (New York: Random House, 1967); C. Taylor, *Sources of Self: The Making of Modern Identity* (Cambridge, MA: Harvard University Press, 1989); P. Young-Eisendrath and J. A. Hall, "Ways of Speaking of Self," in P. Young-Eisendrath and J. A. Hall (eds.), *The Book of the Self: Person, Pretext, and Process* (New York: New York University Press, 1987).

102   Singer: June Singer's books are *The Unholy Bible: Blake, Jung, and the Collective Unconscious* (Boston: Sigo Press, 1986); *Androgyny: The Opposites Within* (Boston: Sigo Press, 1989); *Love's Energies,* 2d ed. (Boston: Sigo Press, 1990); *Seeing through the Visible World: Jung, Gnosis, and Chaos* (Palo Alto, CA: Harper & Row, 1990); *A Gnostic Book of Hours: Keys to Inner Wisdom* (San Francisco: HarperSanFrancisco, 1992); *Boundaries of the Soul: The Practice of Jung's Psychology* (New York: Doubleday, 1994).

104   "From the earliest infantile prostrate self": For theoretical outlines of the stages of self development, see E. Erikson, *Identity and the Life Cycle* (New York: W. W. Norton, 1980); M. Mahler, F. Pine, and A. Bergman, *The Psychological Birth of the Human Infant: Symbiosis and Individuation* (New York: Basic Books, 1975); L. A. Sroufe, "An Organizational Perspective on the Self," in D. Cicchetti and M. Beeghley (eds.), *The Self in Transition: Infancy to Childhood* (Chicago: University of Chicago Press, 1990), pp. 281–307; D. N. Stern, *The Interpersonal World of the Infant* (New York: Basic Books, 1985).

104   "magical thinking": For an overview of the transition from the magical thinking of the preoperational toddler to the logical thought of childhood, see Jean Piaget's theory and research on

cognitive development: *The Language and Thought of the Child,* trans. M. Warden (New York: Harcourt Brace, 1926); *The Child's Conception of the World* (London: Routledge, 1929); *The Moral Judgement of the Child* (New York: Free Press, 1932).

106 "In a large study of people who were resilient": This study captures how the resilient integrate adversity into their self-understanding, providing meaning and purpose to their lives. This recasting of adversity into a positive light is a common theme among the resilient regardless of the type of adversity experienced. See W. Beardslee, "The Role of Self Understanding in Resilient Individuals: The Development of a Perspective," *American Journal of Orthopsychiatry* 59 (1989): 266–278.

111 "Not all cultures": See R. Harré, *Social Being* (Cambridge, England: Blackwell, 1979); R. Harré, *Personal Being: A Theory for Individual Psychology* (Oxford: Basil Blackwell, 1983); P. Kapleau, *Living Zen in America* (New York: Scribner, in press); C. Taylor, *Human Agency and Language: Philosophical Papers,* vol. 1 (Cambridge, England: Cambridge University Press, 1985).

112 Macy: J. Macy, *World as Lover, World as Self* (Berkeley, CA: Parallax Press, 1991), p. 12.

112 "empty center": See note for p. 99 on the self in Jung's theory.

112 "essential self": Essentialist theories assume that personality is founded on biology or some transcendent principle. That is, personality has essential roots outside of social influences.

112 "Although each of us is a center of organized action": The psychoanalyst Margaret Mahler addresses the initial confusion of the infant's physical and later psychological boundaries with the mother. She details the subsequent formation of self-boundaries, culminating around eighteen months of age. See M. Mahler, "On the First Three Subphases of the Separation-Individuation Process," *International Journal of Psychoanalysis* 53 (1972): 333–338; M. Mahler, F. Pine, and A. Bergman, *The Psychological Birth.*

The rudimentary forms of self are addressed by the child developmentalist Daniel Stern. Stern conceptualizes infants as

possessing an emergent self, conceived as "a sense of organization in the process of formation." See D. N. Stern, *The Interpersonal World of the Infant*, p. 38. Because the primary caregiver
helps regulate the infant's biological functioning, the developmentalist Alan Sroufe proposes that the self-organization (including the physiological and emotional regulation of the
infant) resides in the infant-caregiver (dyadic) organization and
not solely in the infant. With development, this coregulation
transforms into self-regulation (Sroufe, "An Organizational Perspective").

113   "birth of self-conscious emotions": The psychologist and researcher Michael Lewis uses the term *secondary emotions* for emotions such as pride or embarrassment that are self-conscious and
self-evaluative. These emotions emerge in the second half of
the second year with the development of a sense of self. See
M. Lewis, *Shame: The Exposed Self* (New York: Free Press, 1991);
M. Lewis et al., "Self Development and Self-Conscious Emotions," *Child Development* 60 (1989): 146–156.

113   "wired up to create a separate self": Because each person is
grounded in a separate physical body, we know self and other
differently, at first on a sensorimotor level and later on a psychological level. See S. Pipp, "Sensorimotor and Repre-
sentational Internal Working Models of Self, Other, and
Relationship: Mechanisms of Connection and Separation," in
D. Cicchetti and M. Beeghly (eds.), *The Self in Transition: Infancy
to Childhood* (Chicago: University of Chicago Press, 1990),
pp. 243–264; D. N. Stern, *The Interpersonal World of the Infant*.

113   Harré: For a discussion of Harré's concept of "individual subjectivity," see R. Harré, *Personal Being*; R. Harré, "The 'Self' as a
Theoretical Concept," in M. Krausz (ed.), *Relativism: Interpretation
and Confrontation* (Notre Dame, IN: University of Notre Dame
Press, 1989).

114   "We develop the function of self": The development of the
function of self, or self-organization, occurs within the context
of our relationships. This relational perspective can be found in

the following works: T. H. Ogden, *The Matrix of the Mind: Object Relations and the Psychoanalytic Dialogue.* (Northvale, NJ: Jason Aronson, 1986); W. F. Overton, "The Arrow of Time and the Cycle of Time: Concepts of Change, Cognition, and Embodiment," *Psychological Inquiry* 5 (1994): 215–237; Sroufe, "An Organizational Perspective"; H. S. Sullivan, *The Interpersonal Theory of Psychiatry* (New York: W. W. Norton, 1953); C. Taylor, "The Dialogical Self," in D. R. Hiley, J. F. Bohman, and R. Shusterman (eds.), *The Interpretive Turn: Philosophy, Science, Culture* (Ithaca, NY: Cornell University Press, 1991).

115   "self does vary a great deal from culture to culture": For a discussion of variations of self across cultures and the reflection of this in language, see R. Harré, *Social Being*; R. Harré, *Personal Being.*

116   Jung: See note for p. 54.

116   "Western societies": Our society's hypervaluing of autonomy is discussed by many feminist theorists of psychology, anthropology, literature, and theology. A recent interesting account comes from a Buddhist scholar, Ann Klein, *Meeting the Great Bliss Queen: Buddhists, Feminists, and the Art of the Self* (Boston: Beacon Press, 1994).

118   "empty center": See note for p. 99 on the self in Jung's theory.

118   Jung: See C. G. Jung, *Memories, Dreams, Reflections* (New York: Vintage Books, 1961), p. 359.

128   *Boundaries of the Soul:* See note for p. 102.

131   Klein: See A. Klein, *Meeting the Great Bliss Queen*, p. 40.

Page   *Part Five*

139   Dharmasiri: See G. Dharmasiri, *Buddhist Ethics* (Antioch, CA: Golden Leaves Publishing, 1989), p. 38.

140   Jung: See note for p. 9.

140   Schafer: See R. Schafer, *Language and Insight* (New Haven: Yale University Press, 1978), pp. 180–181.

141   "capacity to think abstractly": For a description of the development of formal operational thinking (abstract thought) in ado-

lescence, see B. Inhelder and J. Piaget, *The Growth of Logical Thinking from Childhood to Adolescence* (London: Routledge, 1958). Also see D. Elkind, *Child Development and Education: A Piagetian Perspective* (New York: Oxford University Press, 1976); D. Elkind, *The Child and Society: Essays in Applied Child Development* (New York: Oxford University Press, 1979). The magical or omnipotent thinking that permeates the early years of life contributes to the power of our psychological complexes. With the development of self-reflective thought in adolescence, we can reflect on our thinking (and complexes) in terms of coherence, consistency, and lack of contradictions, and the omnipotence and illogicality that characterize complexes can be recognized. In other words, this new form of thought permits us to imagine other possibilities, allowing us to reevaluate the meaning of childhood experiences, and subsequently change complexes rather than *feeling* controlled by them (see W. F. Overton et al., "Formal Operations as Regulatory Context in Adolescence," *Adolescent Psychiatry* [Chicago: University of Chicago Press, 1991]).

146 Shibvon: Shibvon's story is told in Gina Higgins's book *Resilient Adults: Overcoming a Cruel Past* (San Francisco: Jossey-Bass, 1994).

147 "Inherent in each intention": J. Goldstein and J. Kornfield, *Seeking the Heart of Wisdom: The Path of Insight Meditation* (Boston: Shambhala, 1987), p. 111.

150 "transcendent function": The transcendent function, in Jung's words, "is a union of conscious and unconscious contents" that allows a dialectical interplay of different levels or organizations of consciousness. In 1958, Jung wrote a brief commentary for the publication of his 1916 essay "The Transcendent Function" that says this function is "identical with the universal question: How does one come to terms in practice with the unconscious? . . . For the unconscious is not this thing or that; it is the Unknown as it immediately affects us." See C. G. Jung, *The Transcendent Function*, vol. 8 of *The Collected Works of C. G. Jung*, 2d ed., trans. R. F. C. Hull (Princeton, NJ: Princeton University Press, 1959), pp. 67–68. Here Jung is referring to that which

falls outside our capacity to imagine, speak, or fantasize it—the Unknown. Later in the essay he says that "There is nothing mysterious or metaphysical about the term" (transcendent function), and in 1920 he says that this function "facilitates a transition from one attitude to another. The raw material shaped by thesis and antithesis . . . is the living symbol" (see Jung, *The Collected Works*, vol. 6, par. 828). I believe that he is describing the ability to discover something entirely new by holding open the meaning of an event or perception that causes conflict, until one can entertain both (or many) sides of the tension in a new synthesis.

150 "story frequently quoted by Roshi Philip Kapleau": See P. Kapleau, *The Wheel of Life and Death: A Practical Spiritual Guide to Death, Dying, and Beyond* (New York: Doubleday, 1989), p. 247.

152 "potential space": For a discussion by Winnicott of the concept of "potential space" or "play space," see D. W. Winnicott: *The Maturational Process and the Facilitating Environment* (New York: International Universities Press, 1960); *Playing and Reality* (London: Routledge, 1971); *Human Nature* (New York: Schocken Books, 1988).

153 "Dialogue Therapy": My use of dialogue therapy with couples is described in two earlier books: P. Young-Eisendrath, *Hags and Heroes: A Feminist Approach to Jungian Psychotherapy with Couples* (Toronto: Inner City Books, 1984); P. Young Eisendrath, *You're Not What I Expected: Learning to Love the Opposite Sex* (New York: William Morrow, 1993).

155 Ogden: For a discussion of the psychoanalyst Thomas Ogden's term "dialogical space," see T. H. Ogden, *The Matrix of the Mind: Object Relations and the Psychoanalytic Dialogue* (Northvale, NJ: Jason Aronson, 1986). Thomas Ogden emphasizes the "space" between a symbol (a word or image) and an experience (that which is symbolized). Ogden asks us to recognize that a person always fills that space, that a person is creating a response. The response is not creating the person; we're never merely reactive to our environment or experiences. We're always interactive.

Ogden claims that pathologies of the psyche lie mostly in the fantasy that objects or events are things in themselves rather than interpreted by us. Confusion exists, then, about our own subjective states. Under these circumstances, a hallucination does not *sound* like a voice, it *is* a voice. This kind of objectification of psychological states and emotions is typical of serious mental illness and transitory states of shock or confusion. What Ogden alerts us to specifically is the interpreter, the person, who "knows" something through her or his own lens or attitude.

155   Macy: Macy, like others, points to the constructivist theory of meaning; see J. Macy, *World as Lover, World as Self* (Berkeley, CA: Parallax Press, 1991), p. 68.

158   "Zen Bible": See P. Kapleau, *The Three Pillars of Zen* (New York: Doubleday, 1989).

161   "Works Progress Administration": The Works Progress Administration was created in 1935 in the second hundred days of Franklin D. Roosevelt's presidency in order to combat the Great Depression. The administration provided Americans with jobs constructing highways, streets, buildings, parks and other projects intended to have long-range value. It also provided work for artists, writers, actors, and musicians.

161   "Nuremberg trials": Kapleau is referring to the court trials for war criminals of World War II held in Nuremberg, Germany, and in Tokyo, Japan where he served as chief court reporter.

166   Kapleau's five books on Buddhism are *To Cherish all Life: A Buddhist View of Animal Slaughter and Meat Eating* (Rochester, New York: Rochester Zen Center, 1981); *The Three Pillars of Zen* (New York: Doubleday, 1989); *Zen: Merging East and West* (New York: Doubleday, 1989); *The Wheel of Life and Death: A Practical and Spiritual Guide to Death, Dying, and Beyond* (New York: Doubleday, 1990). His next book, *Living Zen in America*, will be published by Scribner, New York, in 1997.

169   "emotions born of body boundaries": For a discussion of the developmental transition from primary human emotions to self-conscious emotions that accompanies the development of the

self, see M. Lewis, *Shame: The Exposed Self* (New York: Free Press, 1991); M. Lewis et al., "Self Development and Self-Conscious Emotions," *Child Development* 60 (1989): 146–156.

170 "Emotions are organizing functions": For a discussion of the adaptive functions of primary emotions, see J. J. Campos and K. C. Barrett, "Toward a New Understanding of Emotions and Their Development," in C. E. Izard, J. Kagan, and R. B. Zajonc (eds.), *Emotions, Cognitions, and Behavior* (New York: Cambridge University Press, 1984); C. Darwin, *The Expression of Emotions in Man and Animals* (Chicago: Chicago University Press, 1965); C. E. Izard, *The Face of Emotion* (New York: Appleton-Century-Crofts, 1971); C. E. Izard, *Patterns of Emotions* (New York: Academic, 1972); C. E. Izard, *Human Emotions* (New York: Plenum, 1977).

170 "envy": My discussion of envy and jealousy draws primarily on a psychoanalytic theory of envy originated by Melanie Klein and on my own clinical experiences. Klein proposed that fantasies about our destructive emotions are universal in human infancy as the infant becomes aware of its dependence on Mother and the separateness of Mother as an individual. For Klein's developmental perspective on envy and jealousy, see M. Klein, *Envy and Gratitude and Other Works* (New York: Delacorte Press, 1975).

174 Tavris: See C. Tavris, *Anger: The Misunderstood Emotion* (New York: Simon & Schuster, 1989).

178 Kapleau: See P. Kapleau, *The Wheel of Life and Death*, p. 267.

179 "the assumption here is that empirical truths": For a history and presentation on the nature of empirical "truth," see W. F. Overton, "World Views and Their Influence on Psychological Theory and Research: Kuhn-Lakatos-Laudan," in H. W. Reese (ed.), *Advances in Child Development and Behavior*, vol. 18 (New York: Academic Press, 1984), pp. 191–226; W. F. Overton, "Historical and Contemporary Perspectives on Developmental Theory and Research Strategies," in R. Downs, L. Liben, and D. Palermo (eds.), *Visions of Aesthetics, the Environment, and Develop-*

Notes

ment: *The Legacy of Joachim Wohlwill* (Hillsdale, NJ: Lawrence Erlbaum, 1991), pp. 263–311; W. F. Overton, "The Structure of Developmental Theory," in H. W. Reese (ed.), *Advances in Child Development and Behavior*, vol. 23 (New York: Academic Press, 1991), pp. 1–37. Basically, there are two metatheoretical positions on the nature of truth. The first perspective is most often referred to as realism. Here, truth is conceived as uncovering something that already exists; meaning is independent of human interpretation. Difficulty in answering certain questions is seen as a reflection of the limitations of our methods or instruments. The second metatheoretical perspective is captured in constructivist theories. Here, truth does not exist independently from humans' understanding of it; truth is constructed by humans. The position that data are never divorced from interpretation is captured in a famous quote by Hanson that all data are "theory laden." See N. R. Hanson, *Patterns of Discovery* (London and New York: Cambridge University Press, 1958).

180   Nagel: See T. Nagel, *The View from Nowhere* (Oxford, England: Oxford University Press, 1986), p. 224.

182   Kapleau: See P. Kapleau, *The Wheel of Life and Death*, p. 245.

183   "complexes": See note for p. 51 on psychological complexes.

183   "repetition compulsions": The term "repetition compulsion" was coined by Sigmund Freud to describe the unconscious repetition of emotional patterns created in early childhood. Freud believed that we are destined to repeat what we've been unable to see consciously. See S. Freud, *Remembering, Repeating, and Working Through*, in vol. 12 of the *Standard Edition of the Complete Psychological Works of Sigmund Freud*, ed. and trans. James Strachey (London: Hogarth Press, 1958).

184   "it is precisely the combination": J. Goldstein and J. Kornfield, *Seeking the Heart of Wisdom*, p. 113.

Page   *Part Six*

187   Kapleau: See P. Kapleau, *Zen Bow* (Rochester, NY: Rochester Zen Center Publication, 1969), p. 3.

Notes

188   "A famous story about the Buddha": This story, here given in my adaptation of it, is a traditional teaching story in Buddhism and appears in many publications.

190   Kramer: See P. Kramer, *Listening to Prozac: A Psychiatrist Explores Anti-Depressant Medication and the Remaking of the Self* (New York: Penguin Books, 1994), p. 247.

BIBLIOGRAPHY

American Association of University Women. *Shortchanging Girls, Shortchanging America*. Washington, DC: Greenberg-Lake, 1991.

Anthony, E. J. "The Syndrome of the Psychologically Invulnerable Child." In A. E. Koupernil (ed.), *The Child in His Family: Children at Psychiatric Risk*. New York: Wiley, 1974.

Anthony, E. J., and Cohler, B. J. (eds.). *The Invulnerable Child*. New York: Guilford Press, 1987.

Anthony, E. J., and Koupernick, C. (eds.). *The Child in His Family*, vol. 2. New York: Wiley, 1973.

Antonovsky, A. *Unraveling the Mystery of Health: How People Manage Stress and Stay Well*. San Francisco: Jossey-Bass, 1987.

Baldwin, A. L., Baldwin, C., and Cole, R. E. "Stress-Resistant Families and Stress-Resistant Children." In J. Rolf, A. S. Masten, D. Cicchetti, K. H. Nuechterlein, and S. Weintraub (eds.), *Risk and Protective Factors in the Development of Psychopathology*. Cambridge, England: Cambridge University Press, 1990.

Baynes, C. F., and Wilhelm, R. *The I Ching: The Richard Wilhelm Translation*. 3d ed. Princeton, NJ: Princeton University Press, 1967.

Beardslee, W. "The Role of Self Understanding in Resilient Individuals: The Development of a Perspective." *American Journal of Orthopsychiatry* 59 (1989): 266–278.

Bibliography

Bleuler, M. *The Schizophrenic Disorders: Long-term Patient and Family Studies.* New Haven: Yale University Press, 1978.

Bowlby, J. *Attachment,* vol. 1. New York: Basic Books, 1982. (Original work published 1969.)

———. *A Secure Base: Parent-Child Attachment and Healthy Human Development.* New York: Basic Books, 1988.

Bretherton, I. "Attachment Theory: Retrospect and Prospect." In I. Bretherton and E. Waters (eds.), *Growing Points of Attachment Theory and Research. Monographs of the Society for Research in Child Development* 501 (1985): 3–104.

———. "Communication Patterns, Internal Working Models, and the Intergenerational Transmission of Attachment Relationships." *Infant Mental Health Journal* 11, no. 3 (1990): 237–252.

Campos, J. J., and Barrett, K. C. "Toward a New Understanding of Emotions and Their Development." In C. E. Izard, J. Kagan, and R. B. Zajonc (eds.), *Emotions, Cognitions, and Behavior.* New York: Cambridge University Press, 1984.

Carver, C. S., and Gaines, J. G. "Optimism, Pessimism, and Postpartum Depression." *Cognitive Therapy and Research* 11, no. 4 (1987): 449–462.

Cohen, N. J. "Sex Differences in Child Psychiatric Outpatients: Cognitive, Personality, and Behavioral Characteristics." *Child Psychiatry and Human Development* 20, no. 2 (1989): 113–121.

Cowen, E. L., Wyman, P. A., Work, W. C., and Parker, G. R. "The Rochester Child Resilience Project: Overview and Summary of First Year Findings." *Development and Psychopathology* 2 (1990): 193–212.

Cox, A. L. "Childhood Adversity and the Successful, Resilient Black Adult: A Retrospective Qualitative Study." Ph.D. diss., Smith College School for Social Work, 1994.

Csikszentmihalyi, M. *The Evolving Self: A Psychology for the Third Millennium.* New York: HarperCollins, 1993.

Dalai Lama. *A Policy of Kindness.* Ithaca, NY: Snow Lion Publications, 1990.

Bibliography

Darwin, C. *The Expression of Emotions in Man and Animals.* Chicago: Chicago University Press, 1965. (Original work published 1872.)

Dharmasiri, G. *Buddhist Ethics.* Antioch, CA: Golden Leaves Publishing, 1989.

Dugan, T. F., and Coles, R. (eds.). *The Child in Our Times: Studies in the Development of Resiliency.* New York: Brunner/Mazel, 1989.

Elkind, D. *Child Development and Education: A Piagetian Perspective.* New York: Oxford University Press, 1976.

———. *The Child and Society: Essays in Applied Child Development.* New York: Oxford University Press, 1979.

Epstein, M. *Thoughts without a Thinker: Psychotherapy from a Buddhist Perspective.* New York: Basic Books,1995.

Erikson, E. *Childhood and Society.* New York: W. W. Norton, 1950.

———. *Identity and the Life Cycle.* New York: W. W. Norton, 1980. (Original work published 1959.)

Fine, S. B. "Resilience and Human Adaptability: Who Rises above Adversity?" *American Journal of Occupational Therapy* 45, no. 6 (1991): 493–502.

Finkelhor, D. "The Sexual Abuse of Children: Current Research Reviewed." *Psychiatric Annals: The Journal of Continuing Psychiatric Education* 17, no. 4 (1987): 233–241.

Finkelhor, D., Hotaling, G., Lewis, I. A., and Smith, C. "Sexual Abuse in a National Survey of Adult Men and Women: Prevalence, Characteristics, and Risk Factors." *Child Abuse and Neglect* 14 (1990): 19–28.

Fisher, L., Kokes, R. F., Cole, R. E., Perkins, P. M., and Wynne, L. C. "Competent Children at Risk: A Study of Well-Functioning Offspring of Disturbed Parents." In E. J. Anthony and B. J. Cohler (eds.), *The Invulnerable Child.* New York: Guilford Press, 1987.

Fowler, G. *Dance of a Fallen Monk: The Twists and Turns of a Spiritual Life.* Reading, MA: Addison-Wesley, 1995.

Freud, S. *Remembering, Repeating and Working Through. The Standard Edition of the Complete Psychological Works of Sigmund Freud,* vol. 12. Ed. J. Strachey. London: Hogarth Press, 1960.

Bibliography

Gardner, E. S. *The Case of the Backward Mule*. New York: William Morrow, 1946.

Garmezy, N. "Vulnerability Research and the Issue of Primary Prevention." *American Journal of Orthopsychiatry* 41 (1971): 101–116.

————. "The Study of Competence in Children at Risk for Severe Psychopathology." In A. E. Koupernick (ed.), *The Child in His Family: Children at Psychiatric Risk*. New York: Wiley, 1974.

————. "Observations of Research with Children at Risk for Child and Adult Psychopathology." In M. McMillan and S. Henao (eds.), *Child Psychiatry: Treatment and Research*. New York: Brunner/Mazel, 1978.

————. "Stress-Resistant Children: The Search for Protective Factors." In J. E. Stevenson (ed.), *Recent Research in Developmental Psychopathology*. New York: Pergamon Press, 1985.

————. "Resiliency and Vulnerability to Adverse Developmental Outcomes Associated with Poverty." *American Behavioral Scientist* 34, no. 4 (1991): 416–430.

Goldstein, J., and Kornfield, J. *Seeking the Heart of Wisdom: The Path of Insight Meditation*. Boston: Shambhala, 1987.

Gottlieb, D. *Family Matters: Healing in the Heart of the Family*. New York: NAL/Dutton, 1991.

Gray, R. E. "Adolescent Response to the Death of a Parent." *Journal of Youth and Adolescence* 16 (1987): 511–525.

Harré, R. *Social Being: A Theory for Social Psychology*. Totowa, NJ: Rowman & Littlefield, 1979.

————. *Personal Being: A Theory for Individual Psychology*. Cambridge, MA: Harvard University Press, 1984.

————. "The 'Self' as a Theoretical Concept." in M. Krausz (ed.), *Relativism: Interpretation and Confrontation*. Notre Dame, IN: University of Notre Dame Press, 1989.

Hauser, S., Vieya, M., Jacobson, A., and Wertlieb, S. "Vulnerability and Resilience in Adolescence: Views from the Family." *Journal of Adolescence* 5, no. 1 (1985): 81–100.

Higgins, G. O. *Resilient Adults: Overcoming a Cruel Past*. San Francisco: Jossey-Bass, 1994.

Bibliography

Holahan, C. J., and Moos, R. H. "Personality, Coping, and Family Resources in Stress Resistance." *Journal of Personality and Social Psychology* 51 (1986): 389–395.

Inhelder, B., and Piaget, J. *The Growth of Logical Thinking from Childhood to Adolescence.* London: Routledge, 1958.

Izard, C. E. *The Face of Emotion.* New York: Appleton-Century-Crofts, 1971.

———. *Patterns of Emotions.* New York: Academic Press, 1972.

———. *Human Emotions.* New York: Plenum, 1977.

Jung, C. G. *The Collected Works of C. G. Jung.* 2d ed., Trans. R. F. C. Hull (Princeton, NJ: Princeton University Press, 1959).

———. *Psychological Types. The Collected Works*, vol. 6.

———. *Two Essays on Analytical Psychology. The Collected Works*, vol. 7.

———. "A Review of the Complex Theory." *The Collected Works*, vol. 8.

———. "The Transcendent Function." *The Collected Works*, vol. 8.

———. *Alchemical Studies. The Collected Works*, vol. 13.

———. *The Practice of Psychotherapy. The Collected Works*, vol. 16.

———. *The Symbolic Life. The Collected Works*, vol. 18.

———. *Memories, Dreams, Reflections.* New York: Random House, 1961.

———. *Letters, 1906–1950.* Princeton, NJ: Princeton University Press, 1973.

———. *Letters, 1951–1961.* Princeton, NJ: Princeton University Press, 1975.

Kapleau, P. *To Cherish All Life: A Buddhist View of Animal Slaughter and Meat Eating.* Rochester, New York: Rochester Zen Center, 1981.

———. *The Three Pillars of Zen.* New York: Doubleday, 1989. (Original work published 1965.)

———. *Zen: Merging East and West.* New York: Doubleday, 1989.

———. *The Wheel of Life and Death: A Practical and Spiritual Guide to Death, Dying, and Beyond.* New York: Doubleday, 1990.

———. *Living Zen in America.* New York: Scribner, in press.

Kaufman, J., and Zigler, E. "Do Abused Children Become Abusive Parents?" *American Journal of Orthopsychiatry* 57, no. 2 (1987): 186–192.

Kaufmann, C., Grunebaum, H., Cohler, B., and Gamer, E. "Superkids:

Competent Children of Psychotic Mothers." *American Journal of Psychiatry* 136, no. 11 (1979): 1398–1402.

Klein, A. *Meeting the Great Bliss Queen: Buddhists, Feminists, and the Art of the Self.* Boston: Beacon Press, 1994.

Klein, M. *Envy and Gratitude and Other Works.* New York: Delacorte Press, 1975.

Kohut, H. *The Analysis of the Self.* New York: International Universities Press, 1971.

———. *The Restoration of the Self.* New York: International Universities Press, 1977.

Kornfield, J. *A Path with Heart: A Guide Through the Perils and Promises of Spiritual Life.* New York: Bantam Books, 1993.

Kramer, P. *Listening to Prozac: A Psychiatrist Explores Anti-Depressant Drugs and the Remaking of the Self.* New York: Penguin Books, 1994.

Krell, R. "Child Survivors of the Holocaust: Strategies of Adaptation." *Canadian Journal of Psychiatry* 38 (1993): 384–389.

Lauterbach, D., and Vrana, S. *Incidence of Traumatic Events and Post-traumatic Psychological Symptoms Among College Students.* Paper presented at the 63d annual meeting of the Midwestern Psychological Association, Chicago, 1991.

Lazarus, R. S. *Emotion and Adaptation.* New York: Oxford University Press, 1991.

Lazarus, R. S., and Folkman, S. *Stress, Appraisal, and Coping.* New York: Springer, 1984.

Lazarus, R. S., Kanner, A. D., and Folkman, S. "Emotions: A Cognitive-Phenomenological Analysis." In R. Pluttchik and H. Kellerman (eds.), *Emotion: Theory, Research, and Experience.* New York: Academic Press, 1980.

Levit, D. B. "Gender Differences in Ego Defenses in Adolescence: Sex Role as One Way to Understand the Differences." *Journal of Personality and Social Psychology* 61, no. 6 (1991): 992–999.

Lewis, M. *Shame: The Exposed Self.* New York: Free Press, 1991.

Lewis, M., Sullivan, M. W., Stanger, C., and Weiss, M. "Self Development and Self-Conscious Emotions." *Child Development* 60 (1989): 146–156.

Bibliography

Luther, S. S. "Vulnerability and Resilience: A Study of High-Risk Adolescents." *Child Development* 62 (1991): 600–616.

Macy, J. *Despair and Personal Power in the Nuclear Age.* Denver: New Social Publishers, 1983.

———. *Dharma and Development: Religion as a Resource in the Sarvodaya Self-Help Movement.* West Hartford, CT: Kumarian Press, 1983.

———. *Mutual Causality in Buddhism and General Systems Theory: The Dharma of Natural Systems.* New York: State University of New York Press. 1991.

———. *World as Lover, World as Self.* Berkeley, CA: Parallax Press, 1991.

Mahler, M., Pine, F., and Bergman, A. *The Psychological Birth of the Human Infant: Symbiosis and Individuation.* New York: Basic Books, 1975.

Martin, R. (ed.) and Morimoto, J. (illus.). *One Hand Clapping: Zen Stories for All Ages.* New York: Rizzoli International Publishers, 1995.

Masten, A. S., Best, K. M., and Garmezy, N. "Resilience and Development: Contributions from the Study of Children Who Overcome Adversity." *Development and Psychopathology* 2 (1990): 425–444.

Masten, A. S., and Garmezy, N. "Risk, Vulnerability, and Protective Factors in Developmental Psychopathology." In B. B. Lahey and A. E. Kazdin (eds.), *Advances in Clinical Child Psychology,* vol. 8. New York: Plenum, 1985.

Masten, A. S., Morison, P., Pellegrini, D., and Tellegen, A. "Competence under Stress: Risk and Protective Factors." In J. Rolf, A. S. Masten, D. Cicchetti, K. H. Nuechterlein, and S. Weintraub (eds.), *Risk and Protective Factors in the Development of Psychopathology.* Cambridge, England: Cambridge University Press, 1990.

Meckel, D. J., and Moore, R. L. *Self and Liberation: The Jung-Buddhism Dialogue.* Mahwah, NY: Paulist Press, 1992.

Moran, P. B., and Eckenrode, J. "Gender Differences in the Costs and Benefits of Peer Relationships during Adolescence." *Journal of Adolescent Research* 6, no. 4 (1991): 396–409.

Muller, W. *Legacy of the Heart: The Spiritual Advantages of a Painful Childhood.* New York: S & S Trade, 1993.

Nagel, T. *The View from Nowhere.* Oxford: Oxford University Press, 1986.

Bibliography

Ogden, T. H. *The Matrix of the Mind: Object Relations and the Psychoanalytic Dialogue.* Northvale, NJ: Jason Aronson, 1986.

O'Grady, D., and Metz, J. R. "Resilience in Children at High Risk for Psychological Disorder." *Journal of Pediatric Psychology* 12, no. 1 (1987): 3–23.

Overton, W. F. "The Structure of Developmental Theory." In H. W. Reese (ed.), *Advances in Child Development and Behavior,* vol. 23. New York: Academic Press, 1991.

———. "The Arrow of Time and the Cycle of Time: Concepts of Change, Cognition, and Embodiment." *Psychological Inquiry* 5 (1994): 215–237.

Perera, S. *Descent to the Goddess: A Way of Initiation for Women.* Toronto, Canada: Inner City Books, 1981.

Piaget, J. *The Language and Thought of the Child.* Trans. M. Warden. New York: Harcourt Brace, 1926.

———. *The Child's Conception of the World.* London: Routledge, 1929.

———. *The Moral Judgment of the Child.* New York: Free Press, 1932.

Radke-Yarrow, M., and Sherman, T. "Hard Growing: Children Who Survive." In J. Rolf, A. S. Masten, D. Cicchetti, K. H. Nuechterlein, and S. Weintraub (eds.), *Risk and Protective Factors in the Development of Psychopathology.* Cambridge, England: Cambridge University Press, 1990.

Rahula, W. *What the Buddha Taught.* New York: Grove Press, 1974.

Ricks, M. "The Social Transmission of Parental Behavior: Attachment across Generations." In I. Bretherton and E. Waters (eds.), *Growing Points of Attachment Theory and Research. Monographs of the Society for Research in Child Development* 501 (1985): 211–230.

Rolf, J., Masten, A. S., Cicchetti, D., Nuechterlein, K. H., and Weintraub, S. (eds.). *Risk and Protective Factors in the Development of Psychopathology.* Cambridge, England: Cambridge University Press, 1990.

Rutter, M. "Sex Differences in Children's Responses to Family Stress." In E. J. Anthony and C. Koupernick (eds.), *The Child in His Family,* vol. 1. New York: Wiley, 1970.

———. "Early Sources of Security and Competence." In J. Bruner and

Bibliography

J. Garten (eds.), *Human Growth and Development*. New York: Oxford University Press, 1978.

————. "Protective Factors in Children's Responses to Stress and Disadvantage." In M. W. Kent and J. Rolf (eds.), *Primary Prevention of Psychopathology*, vol. 3. Hanover, NH: University Press of New England, 1979.

————. "Epidemiological-Longitudinal Approaches to the Study of Development." In W. A. Collins (ed.), *The Concept of Development, Minnesota Symposia on Child Psychology*, vol. 15. Hillsdale, NJ: Lawrence Erlbaum, 1982.

————. "Psychosocial Resilience and Protective Mechanisms." *American Journal of Orthopsychiatry*. 57, no. 3 (1987): 316–331.

————. "Psychosocial Resilience and Protective Factors Mechanisms." In J. Rolf, A. S. Masten, D. Cicchetti, K. H. Nuechterlein, and S. Weintraub (eds.), *Risk and Protective Factors in the Development of Psychopathology*. Cambridge, England: Cambridge University Press, 1990.

Rutter, M., and Quinton, D. "Long-Term Follow-Up of Women Institutionalized in Childhood: Factors Promoting Good Functioning in Adult Life." *British Journal of Developmental Psychology* 2 (1984): 191–204.

Rutter, M., Yule, B., Quinton, D., Rowland, O., Yule, W., and Berger, W. "Attainment and Adjustment in Two Geographical Areas: III. Some Factors Accounting for Area Differences." *British Journal of Psychiatry* 126 (1975): 520–533.

Sadker, M., and Sadker, D. *Failing at Fairness: How America's Schools Cheat Girls*. New York: Macmillan, 1994.

Sameroff, A. J., and Emde, R. N. (eds.). *Relationship Disturbances in Early Childhood: A Developmental Approach*. New York: Basic Books, 1989.

Schaefer, J. A., and Moos, R. H. "Life Crises and Personal Growth." In B. N. Carpenter (ed.), *Personal Coping: Theory, Research, and Applications*. Westport, CT: Praeger, 1992.

Schafer, R. *Language and Insight*. New Haven: Yale University Press, 1978.

Bibliography

Scheier, M. F., Weintraub, J. K., and Carver, C. S. "Coping with Stress: Divergent Strategies of Optimists and Pessimists." *Journal of Personality and Social Psychology* 51, no. 6 (1986): 1257–1264.

Segal, S., and Figley, C. "Stressful Events." *Hospital and Community Psychiatry* 39, no. 9 (1988): 998.

Singer, J. *The Unholy Bible: Blake, Jung, and the Collective Unconscious.* Boston: Sigo Press, 1986.

———. *Androgyny: The Opposites Within.* Boston, MA: Sigo Press, 1989.

———. *Love's Energies.* 2d ed. Boston: Sigo Press, 1990.

———. *Seeing through the Visible World: Jung, Gnosis, and Chaos.* Palo Alto, CA: Harper & Row, 1990.

———. *Gnostic Book of Hours: Keys to Inner Wisdom.* San Francisco: HarperSanFrancisco, 1992.

———. *Boundaries of the Soul: The Practice of Jung's Psychology.* New York: Doubleday, 1994. (Original work published 1973.)

Sogyal, R. *The Tibetan Book of Living and Dying.* San Francisco: HarperSanFrancisco, 1992.

Sroufe, L. A. "An Organizational Perspective on the Self." In D. Cicchetti and M. Beeghley (eds.), *The Self in Transition: Infancy to Childhood.* Chicago: University of Chicago Press, 1990.

Sroufe, L. A., and Fleeson, J. "Attachment and the Construction of Relationships." In W. Hartup and Z. Rubin (eds.), *Relationships and Development.* Hillsdale, NJ: Lawrence Erlbaum, 1986.

Stern, D. N. *The Interpersonal World of the Infant.* New York: Basic Books, 1985.

Sullivan, H. S. *The Interpersonal Theory of Psychiatry.* New York: W. W. Norton, 1953.

———. *The Collected Works of Harry Stack Sullivan, M.D.* Ed. H. S. Perry and M. L. Gawel. New York: W. W. Norton, 1956.

Suzuki, S. *Zen Mind, Beginner's Mind.* New York: Weatherhill, 1970.

Tavris, C. *Anger: The Misunderstood Emotion.* New York: Simon & Schuster, 1989.

Taylor, C. *Human Agency and Language: Philosophical Papers,* vol. 1. Cambridge, England: Cambridge University Press, 1985.

Bibliography

———. *Sources of the Self: The Making of Modern Identity.* Cambridge, MA: Harvard University Press, 1989.

———. "The Dialogical Self." In D. R. Hiley, J. F. Bohman, and R. Shusterman (eds.), *The Interpretive Turn: Philosophy, Science, Culture.* Ithaca, NY: Cornell University Press, 1991.

Vaillant, G. E. *Adaptation to Life.* Boston: Little, Brown, 1977.

Valentine, L., and Feinauer, L. L. "Resilience Factors Associated with Female Survivors of Childhood Sexual Abuse." *American Journal of Family Therapy* 21 (1993): 216–224.

Vaughn, C. E., and Leff, J. P. "The Influence of Family and Social Factors on the Course of Psychiatric Illness." *British Journal of Psychiatry* 129 (1976): 125–137.

Werner, E. E. "High-Risk Children in Young Adulthood: A Longitudinal Study from Birth to 32 Years." *American Journal of Orthopsychiatry* 59, no. 1 (1989): 72–81.

Werner, E. E., and Smith, R. S. *Vulnerable but Invincible: A Study of Resilient Children.* New York: McGraw-Hill, 1982.

Whiteman, D. B. "Holocaust Survivors and Escapees: Their Strengths." *Psychotherapy* 30 (1993): 443–451.

Wilber, K., and Wilber, T. K. *Grace and Grit: Spirituality and Healing in the Life and Death of Treya Killan Wilber.* Boston: Shambhala, 1994.

Winnicott, D. W. *The Maturational Process and the Facilitating Environment.* New York: International Universities Press, 1960.

———. *Playing and Reality.* London: Tavistock, 1971.

———. *Human Nature.* New York: Schocken Books, 1988.

Yarrow, L. "Maternal Deprivation: Toward an Empirical and Conceptual Re-Evaluation." *Psychological Bulletin* 58 (1961): 459–490.

Young-Eisendrath, P. *Hags and Heroes: A Feminist Approach to Jungian Psychotherapy with Couples.* Toronto, Canada: Inner City Books, 1984.

———. *You're Not What I Expected: Learning to Love the Opposite Sex.* New York: William Morrow, 1993.

Young-Eisendrath, P., and Hall, J. A. "Ways of Speaking of Self." In P. Young-Eisendrath and J. A. Hall (eds.), *The Book of the Self: Person, Pretext, and Process.* New York: New York University Press, 1987.

Bibliography

———. Jung's *Self Psychology: A Constructivist Perspective*. New York: Guilford Press, 1991.

Young-Eisendrath, P., and Wiedemann, F. *Female Authority: Empowering Women through Psychotherapy*. New York: Guilford Press, 1987.

INDEX

Index

Index

Index

Index

Index

Index

Index